DISCOVERING FAVOR WITH

GOD

DISCOVERING FAVOR WITH
GOD

SIMPLE
KEYS TO
EXPERIENCING
GOD'S LOVE
FOR YOU

LOREN
COVARRUBIAS

Destiny Image® Publishers, Inc.
P.O. Box 310
Shippensburg, PA 17257-0310

*"Speaking to the Purposes of God for This Generation
and for the Generations to Come"*

ISBN 0-7684-2965-X

For Worldwide Distribution
Printed in the U.S.A.

This book and all other Destiny Image, Revival Press, MercyPlace,
Fresh Bread, Destiny Image Fiction, and Treasure House books are available
at Christian bookstores and distributors worldwide.

1 2 3 4 5 6 7 8 9 10 / 09 08 07 06 05 04

For a U.S. bookstore nearest you, call
1-800-722-6774.

For more information on foreign distributors, call
717-532-3040.

Or reach us on the Internet:
www.destinyimage.com

Dedication

I would like to dedicate this book to the great partners I have in ministry at Mt. Zion. This includes my beloved family, staff and congregation. You have all been so necessary for my journey of faith. Not only have I taught you but you have taught me so much. The love and support I receive is gratefully appreciated. God spoke to me and said, "I will make you a vessel of the new wine and I will give to you a people from whom will flow the wine of the Lord." This word has truly come to pass!

Acknowledgments

I would like to acknowledge and thank my sister Jeanne Cagle for her advice in the writing and editing of this book. Her lifetime knowledge of my thought patterns and her grammatical skills make her help invaluable. Also, thank you to Wendy Halsey for keeping us both on our timetables.

Table of Contents

Chapter One

Father's Plan, Man's Fall, and a Glorious Restoration

The son of Enosh, the son of Seth, the son of Adam, the Son of God (Luke 3:38).

It was 3:00 in the morning when my wife, Bonnie's, water broke. The doctor told us that when the water broke, that would be the signal to call him so that he could meet us at the hospital. Our first child was about to be born. Joy filled our hearts as we thought of all the wonderful implications of having our own child to love and care for. I was 28 and my wife, Bonnie, was 30 when we found out she was pregnant. We had been married almost two years and had known each other for seven. We felt ready and prepared for the next step in our relationship—to have a child. I had already decided I was going to have a son. However, my choice of a son was based more on hope than fact, for Bonnie's pregnancy occurred before the technology of ultrasound took away the mystery of the baby's gender. Nevertheless, I knew I was going to have a child who would carry on my name to future generations. For this reason I was so excited!

The delivery classes had taught me how to minister to my wife when she was going through labor. So with towel and glass of ice chips in hand, I was ready to do my job. But the delivery didn't go as smoothly as the classes we had taken to prepare us for the delivery. Because the labor didn't start immediately, the doctor helped out with a drug called Pitocin. He felt once the water had broken, labor should begin and the baby would soon be born. However, labor brought on in this way can be more intense, and as the day went on, it began to wear on my wife. In fact, she was in labor for 16 hours. It wasn't long before *I* was eating the ice chips and patting *my* head with the towel—not much of a support for my wife as she no longer appreciated my services. I jokingly told her she looked like the girl from The Exorcist, but she wasn't finding my humor or me very funny. Finally, the time of pushing began. It would appear we were at the end of "our" ordeal.

After three hours of pushing, the monitors showed the child was in distress. We had attended one class on caesarean births, but it had never entered our minds it would happen to us, so we really didn't pay much attention to that part of the instruction. In any case, the doctor soon decided he should deliver the child through caesarean section, so off we went to the operating room. It was a strange situation talking to my wife and at the same time seeing the doctor cut her open. I never expected having a child would be so much work!

Finally, out came little Loren. What a rush of joy and excitement at seeing the birth of a child—especially when it's your child! His head was shaped like a football from the ordeal, but he was the most beautiful child God had ever made as far as we were concerned. He was our son! I have to admit my attention quickly changed from my wife to my son. What a joy to hold that bundle of life in my hands for the first time. I can't think of anything greater that I have experienced in my life than that first encounter with the miracle of birth, knowing there was a part of me living in another person. Now I had someone in whom I could invest my hopes, dreams, and my life. More than just my name, I wanted to give him my world.

You've Got Your Father's Eyes

Of course, after a child is born, everyone wants to know who he looks like. There is something about having children that makes the families want to look for themselves in the little one. It is funny to me that we can hate some feature about our looks all our lives and then get excited when we see the same resemblance in our children. "He has my eyes!" "He has Grandma's nose." On down the line we go, looking for those special traits that indicate a certain

superiority of our genes that will be transformed
the next generation. At first, there was a lot of roor
as to who our son really looked like. But after we ...
and watched him grow a little, my wife soon had the upper hand.
She pulled out her baby pictures and showed irrefutable evidence
that this kid looked like her. Now we would wait to see just what
changes maturity would bring in both physical and personal characteristics to indicate who Loren Covarrubias would finally
become. He is now 19 years old, and I have enjoyed observing his
journey with him as well as his two siblings who have joined us in
the journey of life.

THE CREATED SON OF FATHER'S LOVE

As I think about my own son, I can appreciate the day when
God's son, Adam, first entered into the world of God's creation. The
Lord had created a wonderful environment for the son of His love,
including the earth and also the great expanse called the heavens. At
the end of His creative work, Father even patted Himself on the
back and said concerning His creation, "This is good!" Now it was
time for the crowning glory of His creative work. It was time to
make man.

> *Then God said, "Let Us make man in Our image, according to
> Our likeness; let them have dominion over the fish of the sea,
> over the birds of the air, and over the cattle, over all the earth
> and over every creeping thing that creeps on the earth." So God
> created man in His own image; in the image of God He created
> him; male and female He created them* (Genesis 1:26-27).

God was looking for Himself in another person. God could
now have someone in whom He could invest His hopes and dreams
and also His world, and in whom He could trust to accomplish His
purpose. This creature would be different than the others. God
would be able to happily find His own image in this creature, just as
any father would. This creation would become His family, bearing
His image, sharing His world, and living His purpose. This creature
would certainly be God's son.

Even though God would create his son's body from the dust of the earth, he would be different than any other creature in God's earthly creation. The breath that God breathed into Adam was more that just air. This breath of God was filled with life, and as the heavenly breath filled Adam's frame, it awoke the earthly creature giving him life. The life that came from the breath made Adam of the God-kind. This breath or spirit would make him conscious of his heavenly connection. As a spirit man, he would be able to fellowship with God. The life made him conscious of his inner self, hence, creating personality. Man's personality was not the result of his response to external circumstances, but was a reflection emanating from an inner self, related in the image of God.

The spirit of a man is the lamp of the Lord, searching all the inner depths of his heart (Proverbs 20:27).

This creature would be of a spiritual nature. He was more than simple flesh. His true nature lay deep within and could only be explored and understood by the spiritual mind.

For what man knows the things of a man except the spirit of the man which is in him? Even so no one knows the things of God except the Spirit of God (1 Corinthians 2:11).

Man would be a creature of Heaven and also of earth. With his spirit, he was able to link to Heaven, and through his body, he was able to live in the world of man. Like God, he would have the freedom of choice and the ability to reason.

But there is a spirit in man, and the breath of the Almighty gives him understanding (Job 32:8).

How God must have rejoiced as He beheld the man He had created. With great anticipation, He blessed him and gave him authority over all His creation.

Then God blessed them, and God said to them, "Be fruitful and multiply; fill the earth and subdue it; have dominion over the fish of the sea, over the birds of the air, and over every living thing that moves on the earth." And God said, "See, I have given you every herb that yields seed which is on the face of all the earth, and every tree whose fruit yields seed; to you it shall be for food. Also, to every beast of the earth, to every bird of the air, and to everything that creeps on the earth, in which there is life, I have given every green herb for food"; and it was so (Genesis 1:28-30).

IS MAN A GOOD INVESTMENT?

In hindsight, God's investment in man seems like such a bad investment. The psalmist even questioned God in this:

What is man that You are mindful of him, and the son of man that You visit him? For You have made him a little lower than the angels, and You have crowned him with glory and honor. You have made him to have dominion over the works of Your hands; You have put all things under his feet (Psalm 8:4-6).

Wouldn't it seem that angels would have been a better choice than man, in taking charge of God's creation? How can man be compared to angels? The angels have insight and perspective beyond man's perceptions; they have an open access into Heaven; and they possess great power in exercising God's judgments in the world. Indeed, one angel can destroy an army of men or wreak havoc on an entire city. *What is man that God is mindful of him?*

Man was created as a son of God. That's the difference! As any good father will tell you, children are a lot of work, but in the end, you know it's worth the investment. Father's plan for man will not come easily, but the final purpose is worth any divine investment.

You see, it's not about power. God has all the power He needs. It's about relationship. Man was created uniquely to live in relationship with God. Angels were not created after the image and likeness of God; man was. We have been created with the unique insight, personal reflection, and spirit to have this special place with God. Angels were not created for this purpose. They are not worthy of dominion. They are not God's sons. Angels are ministering spirits used by God to minister to us!

But to which of the angels has He ever said: "Sit at My right hand, till I make Your enemies Your footstool"? Are they not all ministering spirits sent forth to minister for those who will inherit salvation? (Hebrews 1:13-14)

Angels were created to serve. Man was created to rule with God. What a difference! This is why God now dispatches His servants, the angels, to minister to and for us. When Jesus came to the earth, He emphasized our need to have the heart and attitude of a servant. Yet, we must understand that although serving is to be our heart attitude, to serve is not our destiny. It is only a pathway to our destiny, and no other pathway will work. He who has not learned to serve will not be able to rule. Our destiny is to rule and reign with Christ, and learning to be a servant is our preparation for the authority to rule. When we mature past childhood, the Father will confer great authority on us.

Now I say that the heir, as long as he is a child, does not differ at all from a slave, though he is master of all, but is under guardians and stewards until the time appointed by the father. Even so we, when we were children, were in bondage under the elements of the world. But when the fullness of the time had come, God sent forth His Son, born of a woman, born under the law, to redeem those who were under the law, that we might receive the adoption as sons (Galatians 4:1-5).

Sadly, many people who have a heart to serve will not come to the place of authority God wants to bring them. The frustration of this slavery mentality will ultimately cause some to drop out of the house of God rather than abide until their fullness comes.

And a slave does not abide in the house forever, but a son abides forever. Therefore if the Son makes you free, you shall be free indeed (John 8:35-36).

A TRAGIC FALL

Unfortunately, God's joy in His creation was short-lived. Man did not fully comprehend his awesome place and position in God. Instead, he rebelled against God and His plan. Man thought that taking his own way, independent of God, would be the source of satisfaction in this life. He saw it as a shortcut, but it was a shortcut that led to a dead end. The end result of man's sin in the garden was that man was cut off from fellowship with God and lost the place God had for him. He died that day in the garden. He didn't die physically, but spiritually.

In many ways, he would revert back to an animalistic life robbed of his great glory in the garden. His life would degenerate into a pursuit of survival in this world, rather than purpose, and he became unaware of the great position God wanted for his sons. All too soon, man's pursuit of life apart from God would bring a very long history of war and suffering.

Fortunately, God didn't despair in the face of this tragic fall. Instead, He made a promise to man. Right in the middle of the curse, there was a promise of a future blessing that would reverse the curse. Mankind could fail their Father, but their Father could not and would not fail them. He promised to bring forth the seed of promise in another day.

> So the Lord God said to the serpent: *"Because you have done this, you are cursed more than all cattle, and more than every beast of the field; on your belly you shall go, and you shall eat dust all the days of your life.* **And I will put enmity between you and the woman,** *and between your seed and her Seed;* **He shall bruise your head,** *and you shall bruise His heel"* (Genesis 3:14-15, emphasis added).

God would again have a Son who would bring forth many sons. This Son would not be discouraged nor fail until He had done the will of His Father and brought man back to his original place in the family of God. He would serve the purposes of Father and then He would rule when those purposes had been accomplished. His life would set the pattern for all future sons. The Son would come and produce a race of the "God-kind" created in their Father's image. They would arise in the glory of their Father and be fruitful and multiply, and fill up the earth with the glory of God. These sons would have dominion, and the purposes of God would be complete in the earth as they followed Father's lead. Because God had decided, it would most certainly happen.

> *Then Job answered the Lord and said: "I know that You can do everything, and that no purpose of Yours can be withheld from You"* (Job 42:1-2).

Chapter Two

A Nurturing Mother and the Favor of God

And the angel answered and said to her, "The Holy Spirit will come upon you, and the power of the Highest will overshadow you; therefore, also, that Holy One who is to be born will be called the Son of God" (Luke 1:35).

In the beginning when the earth was without form and void, and darkness was upon the face of the deep, the Spirit moved upon the waters. The Spirit was preparing the dark world to receive the Word and initiate the great creative acts of God. Then it came. The Lord said, "Let there be light," and there was light. The combination of Spirit and Word brought forth a brand-new world as an environment for the purposes of God.

In a sense, after the sin of Adam, the whole world lived in a similar dark and meaningless void. Spiritual darkness cast a great shadow over the face of the earth, and the world laid waste for millennia because of the sin of Adam. Only in an isolated area of the world, among a few people, was there any real knowledge of the living God. Truly, darkness was upon the nations. But God began to move once again—a light would shine in this deep darkness.

The people who sat in darkness have seen a great light, and upon those who sat in the region and shadow of death light has dawned (Matthew 4:16).

GOD'S WORD TO A YOUNG MAIDEN

His Word would once again cause light to shine upon this dark world, a light that would light up the race of man. The Word of the Lord came through an angel to a young maiden named Mary.

And having come in, the angel said to her, "Rejoice, highly favored one, the Lord is with you; blessed are you among women!" But when she saw him, she was troubled at his saying, and considered what manner of greeting this was. Then the angel said to her, "Do not be afraid, Mary, for you have found favor with God. And behold, you will conceive in your womb and bring forth a Son, and shall call His name Jesus. He will be great, and will be called the Son of the Highest; and the Lord God will give Him the throne of His father David. And He will reign over the house of Jacob forever, and of His kingdom there will be no end" (Luke 1:28-33).

What a frightening experience this must have been for this young maiden! When reading the story of Mary's part in the plan and purposes of God, we see that often Mary only partially understood what God was doing. (God speaks, but does man understand?) There was the supernatural message to Mary, but there had to be a response based upon her perception of that word. It is clear that Mary did not understand because she was not able to perceive the "supernatural," only the natural. Mary asked the heavenly messenger how she could have a child when she was a virgin. The angel of the Lord said:

And the angel answered and said to her, "The Holy Spirit will come upon you, and the power of the Highest will overshadow you; therefore, also, that Holy One who is to be born will be called the Son of God (Luke 1:35).

The Son of God would enter the world of man and once again cause the spiritual world to merge into the natural world. Once again, a man would come to life through the breath of God, the Holy Spirit. Father's breath would bring forth an extraordinary life in this young maiden. Once again, Heaven had a child on the earth, prepared to fulfill the Father's desire for a Son. Truly, Mary found favor with God and was chosen to be a part of this great plan of redeeming man and initiating the purposes of God.

Because there cannot be a son without a mother, it would be in the womb of the woman bearing the precious Seed that would eventually crush the head of satan. Now would be the time for the second Adam to rectify all that the first had lost in the great fall. This Son would usher in a new beginning for the earth, and God would be glorified through His Son.

ACCORDING TO YOUR WORD

How precious and wonderful was Mary's reply to the angel of the Lord.

> *Then Mary said, "Behold the maidservant of the Lord! Let it be to me according to your word." And the angel departed from her* (Luke 1:38).

Yet, I am sure she wasn't prepared for all the trouble this act of obedience would bring her. After she became pregnant, Joseph was deeply troubled and was about to put her away.

> *Now the birth of Jesus Christ was as follows: After His mother Mary was betrothed to Joseph, before they came together, she was found with child of the Holy Spirit* (Matthew 1:18).

What should he do? Put her away as the law prescribed, or take her as his wife as his love demanded? It took a miraculous dream from God to get Joseph to make the right decision. This story is told in only a few verses of Scripture, but I am sure for Mary and Joseph there was a volume of pain and suffering as each agonized over the situation created by this miraculous event.

When it came time for the child to be born, Joseph and Mary had to journey to a faraway city so that Joseph could be a part of a census in Bethlehem, the place of his birth. Of course, 2000 years later we understand that this was simply God's way of getting Mary and Joseph to the place where the prophecies declaring the location of the birth of the Messiah could be fulfilled.

There is a powerful spiritual truth that lies behind this event. Often, hidden in the background, there are divine purposes being worked out in the midst of our distresses. We agonize over our problems, not knowing what is happening in Father's world.

Once they finally arrived in Bethlehem, they were confronted with a city teeming with other pilgrims. At their last stop of the day, they found that there was no room for them in the inn. But the owner graciously consented to allow the couple to stay in the stable. At least in the stable, they would be protected from the outside environment.

AROMA OF HEAVEN, STENCH OF EARTH

The season was just right for the arrival of the child. He was born in a stable, and his crib was a manger. The word *manger* is a glorified name for a feeding trough. How we hate to admit God is at work in uncomfortable circumstances. Yet at times, God hides Himself in simplicity when He is doing something supernatural. God was hidden away in a feeding trough while the world went about its business unaware that God was about to answer the cry of His people. The answer was hidden away in a dirty old stable.

Here was the child of promise, the Son of God, born in such a simple and natural way. In the meantime, out in the fields outside the city, some shepherds were having a heavenly encounter. Immediately, they came into the city to tell Mary they had heard the announcement of the birth of Messiah through a host of angels.

Mary wasn't sure if she should be listening for the angels or figuring out a way to protect her newfound infant from the unsanitary conditions in the stable. A stable full of filthy animals wasn't the most sanitary place for a child to be born. You can be sure Mary's mothering instincts were at work just as strong or stronger than her spiritual senses.

And suddenly there was with the angel a multitude of the heavenly host praising God and saying: "Glory to God in the highest, And on earth peace, goodwill toward men!" (Luke 2:13-14)

Mary, are you going to hear the angels sing, or are you going to be overwhelmed by the aroma of the manure in the stable? Will you step away from your surrounding environment and just listen to the sounds of the heavenly and earthly messengers? The aroma of Heaven is in this place, but will you be able to ignore the stench of the manure? The Lord's miracles are so often hidden under the smell of manure. You see, wherever there is life, there is manure. God's work and ways can be a little dirty at times. Life always has a by-product. There are always the natural processes that accompany the spiritual. We don't usually wear out from the spiritual aspects of our experiences; we wear out from the accompanying manure—in other words, from the natural processes that accompany them. It is often the regular routines of life that wear us out and prevent us from sensing the spiritual realities all around us.

Mothers are the ones who have the primary responsibility of this job. That's why I believe Mary was probably focused on the need at hand more than the song from above. Mary was not going to be a vital part of Jesus' life forever. Her major function was to be His mother. Later, on the cross, Jesus showed His love and concern for her by commissioning John to take care of her. She would certainly be in the upper room to receive the Holy Spirit on the day of Pentecost. Yet, when Jesus was ministering as the Son of God, He had to separate Himself from the bond of His mother to fulfill the will of His Father.

> *And it was told Him by some, who said, "Your mother and Your brothers are standing outside, desiring to see You." But He answered and said to them, "My mother and My brothers are these who hear the word of God and do it"* (Luke 8:20-21).

THE CITY OF GOD—THE MOTHER OF US ALL

The sons of God born today have a mother too. All sons are conceived from the seed of the father but are born and nurtured through a mother. This mother is the City of God.

> *And of Zion it will be said, "This one and that one were born in her; and the Most High Himself shall establish her." The Lord will record, when He registers the peoples: "This one was born there." Selah* (Psalm 87:5-6).

This mother is also called the New Jerusalem:

> *For this Hagar is Mount Sinai in Arabia, and corresponds to Jerusalem which now is, and is in bondage with her children but*

the Jerusalem above is free, which is the mother of us all. For it is written: "Rejoice, O barren, you who do not bear! Break forth and shout, you who are not in labor! For the desolate has many more children than she who has a husband" (Galatians 4:25-27).

The Church collectively is called the mother in the family of God. She is also called the Bride of Christ. The Old Testament people of God were also spoken of in terms of being the wife of God. It was this woman that John, the beloved, saw in Revelation 12.

Now a great sign appeared in heaven: a woman clothed with the sun, with the moon under her feet, and on her head a garland of twelve stars. Then being with child, she cried out in labor and in pain to give birth....She bore a male Child who was to rule all nations with a rod of iron. And her Child was caught up to God and His throne (Revelation 12:1-2,5).

In this day, we will see the fulfillment of these prophecies. There will be a faithful bride and mother who will bring forth a male or man-child who will fulfill the purposes of their Father. We saw this in type when Jesus, the firstborn, was born from the wife of God—Israel, the natural seed of Abraham. He ascended to Heaven and sits on the throne of God. Now, we will see the appearing of the sons of God, born from the New Testament Bride, the Church. These sons will also have authority granted to them because of their faithfulness.

And he who overcomes, and keeps My works until the end, to him I will give power over the nations—"He shall rule them with a rod of iron; they shall be dashed to pieces like the potter's vessels"—as I also have received from My Father (Revelation 2:26-27).

SONS WHO ARE A BRIDE

This is a great irony. Collectively we are called to be the Bride of Christ, but individually, we are called to be the sons of God. We must be responsible for both aspects of our calling if we are to see the fullness of God's Word come to pass. As men in the Church, we must be stretched to understand the feminine aspects of our calling. As women in the church, we need to be stretched to fulfill the masculine aspects of our calling. We live in a day when gender issues in the secular society could easily blur our understanding of the call and purpose of God in the earth. We must be careful neither to blend the roles so they lose their distinction, nor can we stifle one to the detriment of the other. God, in the beginning, created us male and female and together we will take our proper place of dominion!

So God created man in His own image; in the image of God He created him; male and female He created them. Then God blessed them, and God said to them, "Be fruitful and multiply; fill the earth and subdue it; have dominion..." (Genesis 1:27-28).

As it was with Jesus Christ, so it is for the sons of God in our day. The sons must have a mother. We need the mother's willingness to roll up her sleeves and get into the nitty-gritty of everyday life with the people of God preparing them for their great calling in God. The mother's role is not the same as the Father's. The Church, as the mother, has a great responsibility in the plans and purposes of God. Yet, the mother must realize her responsibility is not an end in itself but a preparation for the children of God to grow to maturity and to become the sons of God in the earth.

Paul powerfully provides the distinction for us in his letter to Thessalonians:

But we were gentle among you, just as a nursing mother cherishes her own children. So, affectionately longing for you, we were well pleased to impart to you not only the gospel of God, but also our own lives, because you had become dear to us (1 Thessalonians 2:7-8).

In order for the Church to go on to maturity, it is necessary for her to be able to walk in the balance of divine truth. There are times when God's people need that gentle, nourishing care that a mother would provide her son. We need to see the balance of the Father and the mother, the king and the priest, the son and the bride, the natural and the spiritual, the Word and the Spirit.

Truth is like a coin—it always has more than one side. God's truth is that way. Have you ever wondered why the Word is filled with so many seemingly contradictory ideas? We can learn of the "irresistible" grace of God to call us to Himself, but we also need to learn about our responsibility to properly respond to His call. The Bible says, "Therefore consider the goodness and the severity of God" (Rom. 11:22a). Unfortunately, most of us choose to walk on only one side of truth rather than both sides of truth. Because of our immaturity and traditional teachings, we tend to take sides and make truth one-sided, thus losing the power of the seemingly opposing truth that holds it in tension. Instead of taking sides, we need to take a more spiritually mature perspective that will allow us to view the truths of God from their many sides. The natural mind desires to have "cognitive dissonance." This means we always have to resolve conflicting concepts in our mind. The spiritual mind must operate at a higher level. We must embrace the totality of truth and accept by faith those things we cannot understand or reconcile with natural reasoning. This will only happen as we open our spirits to all God has for us!

THE MOTHER'S ROLE AND THE FATHER'S ROLE

What is the difference between the role of the father and the role of the mother in regards to the children? We must go to the Word for the response.

> *My son, hear the instruction of your father, and do not forsake the law of your mother; for they will be a graceful ornament on your head, and chains about your neck* (Proverbs 1:8-9).

The role of the mother is more personal and also more inclusive. The word "law" in this context is the word *torah*. It is the word used to describe the law of Moses. It has to do with regulatory laws that direct our everyday life. The word "instruction" has the connotation of a warning or chastisement. This is the word we associate with the father. A mother generally has a more personal connection with the child. Her concerns are more specific and detailed. Moms tend to be more concerned with right and wrong and proper behavior, details the father doesn't even always notice. I know in raising

26

my children, my wife concerned herself with things I didn't even see. On more than one occasion, she was giving me the evil eye for not correcting the kids or not enforcing her laws.

Unfortunately, I was also guilty of breaking those laws. As a man, I often have my wife acting as a mother telling me what is right and proper when I just want to move on, oblivious to what is happening around me. While it seems fathers want to put a crown on the children's head and send them out in life, the mom often tends to put a chain around their necks and hold them close. How hard it must have been for Mary when she went after Jesus with the noose one more time and He cut the rope.

At the marriage supper in Cana at the beginning of His minsitry, Jesus was bound by His mother's wish to give the wedding guests some wine. He didn't think it was His time, but His mother wasn't concerned about that. She was overwhelmed by the embarrassment that could be created by this situation. She just wanted Him to show everyone what a good son she had. A mother's love is deep and can induce great pride when her children succeed, but it also can evoke extreme pain when the children go astray.

The father, on the other hand, develops a different bond with the children. He is looking for his children to make him proud but is not likely to embrace the shame if they don't. Women have a tendency to take things more personally. A wayward child makes her feel like *she* was a bad mother. A wayward child makes the father think *he* has a bad *child*.

The proverbs of Solomon: A wise son makes a glad father, but a foolish son is the grief of his mother (Proverbs 10:1).

In the gender blending of our society, we try to blur and blend the differences between men and women. In the Church, we must not allow this to happen for we understand God made us different for a reason. Our differences are our strengths, and when diminished, they become our weaknesses. Like truth, we often stand in opposition, yet, only when we stand together will the Lord have His way. We need the expression of both sides to accurately perceive the truth. We certainly need both men and women exercising ministry in the Church for the fullness of the Bride to be made manifest for her sons to come forth in the earth.

The Church must see her role as the Bride of Christ and also as the mother of the children of God. Within her mothering wings, the Church should nurture and bond with the children. We must give them laws to train them, but also remember that we are not training them for eternal childhood, but for mature sonship. We must be willing to break the chains and release the children to their Father so He can bring them to maturity. As Paul said, the law is only a tutor to bring us to Christ (Gal. 4:1-5 KJV). When the tutor's job is done, he recedes into the background so that the son can move forward.

We also need the ministry of fathers in the Church who speak a word over the sons releasing them to minister to God. This is the true ministry of the apostle—true fathers bringing a word of maturity to release the Body to the fullness that is in God. The Church is in dire need of fathers, like Paul, to not only beget children, but understand how to raise them to maturity and release them to their full purpose in God.

SERVANTHOOD LEADS TO THE THRONE

You are not ready for the Father if you haven't proven yourself with the mother. You are not ready to be a king unless you've learned what it means to be a servant. Jesus Himself was subject to the law of His parents. This was the proving ground making Him ready for His ministry as the Son of God.

Then He went down with them and came to Nazareth, and was subject to them, but His mother kept all these things in her heart. And Jesus increased in wisdom and stature, and in favor with God and men (Luke 2:51-52).

This same example was evident in the life of the great prophet, Samuel, who submitted himself to the law of Eli, which brought his promotion and allowed him to become the prophet over Israel.

And the child Samuel grew in stature, and in favor both with the Lord and men (1 Samuel 2:26).

It was also the pattern established in the early Church.

So continuing daily with one accord in the temple, and break-ing bread from house to house, they ate their food with gladness and simplicity of heart, praising God and having favor with all the people. And the Lord added to the church daily those who were being saved (Acts 2:46-47).

Growing in favor with God should have a corresponding growth of favor with people. It is certain you will not find favor with all people, but you will find favor with those looking for God or those simply benefiting from your service. When you walk with God, you will bear fruit that will attract hungry people.

The fruit of the righteous is a tree of life, and he who wins souls is wise (Proverbs 11:30).

We must understand that this fruit is the by-product of seek-ing the favor of God. Our desire should be to please God, not to be a man-pleaser. You must establish yourself not as a man-pleaser but as a God-pleaser. You must establish yourself not as a servant of the people, but as with Moses, a servant *of God* to the people. Once we have learned how to be a servant, the Father is ready to make us a son. Once we have learned to be a priest, God is ready to make us a king. Once we have learned to serve, God is ready to teach us how to reign. Truly, this is the day for the people of God to arise in the earth with God's great favor. Once we learn to be a proper child, God will be able to make us His proper sons. When we are born again, we are the children of God, but God has more for us.

Beloved, now we are children of God; and it has not yet been revealed what we shall be, but we know that when He is revealed, we shall be like Him, for we shall see Him as He is. And everyone who has this hope in Him purifies himself, just as He is pure (1 John 3:2-3).

A PERSONAL WORD

My own spiritual experience, like Timothy of the Bible, came from the faith of my mother. I had a good mother who taught me of the things of God, and it was from my mother's perspective that I learned of God. I learned the comfort of constant love and care. I knew with my mother I always had someone who cared about me and was sensitive to my needs and desires. My mom taught me to take all my needs and desires to God—there wasn't anything too small for God. He was a God who cared about how I felt. From this early teaching, I developed a strong bond with the Father that has lasted a lifetime.

Although my dad was not active in my spiritual development, he made a tremendous contribution as well. From his strength and strong will, I learned about authority and submission that was easily transferred to my spiritual life. I learned from my relationship with my father the need to give honor and respect to those in authority. I never struggled with having a healthy fear of the Lord nor did I struggle with following the path of righteousness. I know by experience that these are wonderful lessons. They have brought great blessings to my life. I was submissive to my parents, my teachers, my employers, and of course, my spiritual leaders. Honoring those who had rule over me was easy. I experienced many good things from this walk, but God showed me it was just the beginning.

GROWING UP IN THE LORD

The Lord began to show me there was more to my walk than the few lessons I had learned from my parents. I had a foundation, but it was time to build on this foundation. It was time to grow into the fullness of the Father's desire for my life. To get to this place, I would have to change my attitude toward my Father in Heaven. I had to become more released into His hands. I would have to learn more about being a son by seeing who I was in my Father. It is only when we clearly see the Father that we can understand and assume our role as the sons of God in the earth.

Then Jesus answered and said to them, "Most assuredly, I say to you, the Son can do nothing of Himself, but what He sees the Father do; for whatever He does, the Son also does in like manner. For the Father loves the Son, and shows Him all things that He Himself does; and He will show Him greater works than these, that you may marvel" (John 5:19-20).

30

We must move beyond the mother's love to the Father's love. We don't abandon our former understanding, but we must certainly build on it!

Chapter Three

God, Give us Fathers

When He had been baptized, Jesus came up immediately from the water; and behold, the heavens were opened to Him, and He saw the Spirit of God descending like a dove and alighting upon Him. And suddenly a voice came from heaven, saying, "This is My beloved Son, in whom I am well pleased" (Matthew 3:16-17).

Time has slowly and arduously passed since Adam fell from his place of relationship as a son of God on the earth. During the thousands of years that followed, the ancient civilizations have endured wars, plagues, forced slavery, devastation, and treachery. When the time was just right, God unleashed His plan of recovery. The plan would center in the gift of His Son. At His baptism in the Jordan, He announced that He loved this Son and was very pleased with Him. It was as though God was saying, "Son, I am proud of you!" How awesome!

Although the angels are created beings that have a special place in Heaven and they are quick to carry out Father's will, they are not like man. Man is uniquely created in Father's image. Moses and Abraham were the friends of God. Many others were called His servants. The children of Israel were even called His wife, but no one until now could be spoken of as the Son of God!

A FATHER AFFIRMS HIS SON

Jesus came to restore that relationship between Father and His sons. In Christ, we have a man who came to the earth in the image and likeness of God. Fulfilling the Father's will, He could now take

33

a place of dominion, restoring man back to his original place of favor with His Father.

It is important to notice that this affirmation from the Father was not given to Jesus as soon as He came to earth. The approval of the Father would come after the Son had proven Himself worthy of this affirmation. The love of the Father is unconditional, but His approval is not. Many people today think that love and approval are synonymous terms. This is not the case. As it pertains to the love of God, we can be sure that it is unconditional and everlasting. Jesus said if someone is in the palm of God's hand, he cannot be plucked out. God doesn't give up on His kids. His mercy is everlasting and endures forever. However, we should never think God's love means God's approval. To have the seal of the Father's approval, you must be willing to submit yourself to His hand. God loves us. However, to be His sons with an inheritance, we must ascend higher than the love, based upon pure relationship as sons, to the approval, based upon our loving obedience to His will. This approval comes by submitting our lives to the hand of God and allowing Him to bring us to maturity. To find favor in the face of God, one must submit willingly and lovingly to the hand of God.

> For whom the Lord loves He chastens, and scourges every son whom He receives. **If you endure chastening, God deals with you as with sons;** for what son is there whom a father does not chasten? But if you are without chastening, of which all have become partakers, then you are illegitimate and not sons (Hebrews 12:6-8, emphasis added).

The reason the Body of Christ has been able to live only in the realm of servanthood is because we are unwilling to go on to maturity in God. Because we are just children, the Father must deal with us as servants and not sons. The Word declares the "child" of God or the immature son is no different than a servant:

> Now I say that the heir, as long as he is a child, does not differ at all from a slave, though he is master of all, but is under guardians and stewards until the time appointed by the father (Galatians 4:1-2).

The Father wants to give us our inheritance as sons, but we settle on being servants. We cling to our childhood. We want God to be our daddy, but we don't want Him to be our Father. The Scriptures teach us He must be both in order for us to receive our inheritance.

> *And because you are sons, God has sent forth the Spirit of His Son into your hearts, crying out, "Abba, Father!" Therefore you are no longer a slave but a son, and if a son, then an heir of God through Christ* (Galatians 4:6-7).

A DADDY AND A FATHER

When my son was born, I loved being a daddy. My children called me "Pa-pa." It always warmed my heart when I heard it. I am glad to say God has been my "abba," or "papa" using a more modern term. When I was just a kid, God came into my life in a very personal way, and I had an intimate and personal relationship with Him. I was a very sensitive child and very easily intimidated by the things of life, so when I met God through Jesus Christ, I saw God as my shepherd protector. He was the gentle Savior who would comfort me in times of trouble and hold me in times of need. God was my daddy. I had an earthly dad, but God was with me at all times and provided the extra help I needed in life. Truly, I loved Him with my whole heart.

A daddy is like a mother, in that you run to him when you're afraid; you seek His comfort when you feel lonely and vulnerable. His goal is your comfort and your security. Like a mother, daddy is on standby at all times and is careful not to let you suffer pain or discomfort. I loved that role with my children. It was a great feeling to know they wanted me, needed me, and couldn't face life unless they knew I was close by. What an ego booster "daddyhood" can be!

However as a father, I understand that I can't be just a daddy to my children. Another one of the father's roles in the family is to empower his children. My children need me, but I must be willing to wean them away from my strength and help them to develop strength for themselves. My goal should be to bring them to a place of independence so they can go on and do for another generation what I have done for them. As a father, I can't be just what they want me to be; I must also be what they need me to be. I must be willing to let them suffer, if necessary, to learn the trials of life so they will come to a place of maturity.

"Daddyhood" is very popular in our contemporary society, but the concept of fatherhood has fallen on hard times. Maternal instincts have prevailed, and we have a generation of fathers who are afraid to be real fathers. Sometimes it is self-seeking. To be a real father, you have to be willing to be unpopular. You can't always come to the rescue, and sometimes you have to be willing to let your children suffer pain. The impact of liberalism and socialism on the world has convinced people in authority that they are responsible to take away suffering and pain at all costs. What we have created is a welfare state that perpetuates immaturity and dependence rather than maturity and independence. God promises to send a much-needed revival to change this mind-set in the world!

> *Behold, I will send you Elijah the prophet before the coming of the great and dreadful day of the Lord. And he will turn the hearts of the fathers to the children, and the hearts of the children to their fathers, lest I come and strike the earth with a curse* (Malachi 4:5-6).

A Priestly Son Who Suffers With Us

Most of us think that the real suffering of Jesus began when He went to the cross. This is not the case. To fulfill the Father's purpose in the earth and for His eternal destiny as an intercessor for the people of God, Jesus had to go through life, like all humans, experiencing many things. He understood the devastating power of rejection and ridicule. He experienced the pain of personal agony as He observed the sin and sickness of God's people. He suffered at the hands of the religious leaders. He was called to be a high priest who could be deeply moved by our own weaknesses and failures. His future intercession on behalf of man would be made with a true understanding of our pain and distress.

The Scriptures tell us that when Jesus saw the affliction of the people, He was moved with compassion. The word *compassion* means to feel the passion of another person—to be moved deeply in the inward parts of one's being because of the hurts of others. How can we feel compassion? Our life's experiences enable us to feel more deeply the hurt of others and enable us to relate to their problems and their pain. This was the only way Jesus could be a real intercessor. He had to be in touch with our pain. The power in Jesus' hands when He reached out to touch others flowed from His inward parts that had been affected by our condition. Compassion moves the hand of God.

Isaiah 53 gives us insight into the life of Jesus. Many people think that when Jesus was a kid, He was like Superman. He walked around with supernatural powers, using them for His own delight without fully exposing Himself. Some have even claimed to have "lost gospels" telling the stories of Jesus' supernatural youth. The real truth is, at the marriage festival at Cana of Galilee, the miracle ministry of Jesus began. It was here He established Himself and began His ministry as the Son of God in the earth. Isaiah tells us the true story:

> *Who has believed our report? And to whom has the arm of the Lord been revealed? For He shall grow up before Him as a tender plant, and as a root out of dry ground. He has no form or comeliness; and when we see Him, there is no beauty that we should desire Him. He is despised and rejected by men, a Man of sorrows and acquainted with grief. And we hid, as it were, our faces from Him; He was despised, and we did not esteem Him. Surely He has borne our griefs and carried our sorrows; yet we esteemed Him stricken, smitten by God, and afflicted* (Isaiah 53:1-4).

CAN YOU BELIEVE THIS REPORT?

Isaiah begins by saying, "Who will believe our report?" It is unbelievable to us, but Jesus didn't have a picture-perfect childhood. To begin with, Jesus was born into controversy because of His supernatural conception. Most assumed that Mary was having an affair. Even Joseph, His earthly father, may have had some lingering doubts. Knowing what people are like, I have found we all question from time to time the things God has spoken to us. Why would we think Joseph was any different?

Jesus' roots or His genealogy was described as being "a root out of dry ground" (Isa. 53:2). He appeared out of the parched earth that was thirsty for a little drink from Heaven. He was not born in the midst of spiritual renewal. His physical stature and appearance were undesirable. There was no physical sign that made Him attractive to others. No wonder Isaiah said, "Who will believe our report?" I have trouble believing this report myself. If I were God and could have chosen my own body, I would have done better than that. I would have looked like a model from *GQ* magazine! Boy, would I be built! And I would have Him born in a king's palace, certainly no innkeeper's stable. Jesus, however, couldn't be afforded this luxury. His body and His life had to put Him in touch with the reality that the rest of the world lived in. His attraction did not come from His flesh but arose from deep within His spirit.

> *Therefore, when He came into the world, He said: "Sacrifice and offering You did not desire, but a body You have prepared for Me.... Then I said, 'Behold, I have come—in the volume of the book it is written of Me—to do Your will, O God' "* (Hebrews 10:5,7).

DEALING WITH YOUR PAST

I am certain that some of you have not come to terms with your life as a child. *Why did I have to go through the things I did? Why couldn't I have had loving parents? Why was I rejected in school? Why couldn't I get good grades? Why was I abused?* Some may have even suffered cruelty from others because you were different—maybe they didn't like the way you looked or the clothes you wore. I know growing up, life could have been different, maybe easier for you. But who knows how your experiences have uniquely prepared you for the Father's eternal purpose that He has designed for your life?

I know when I was young, I never could figure out how people could throw a ball and let go at the same time. No wonder I was always the last one to be picked for the teams. I was the one they fought over *not* to be on their team! I have found, however, that all my experiences have created me in a way that the Lord can use me in very special ways. I know for sure that my weaknesses have forced me to reach out to God more than others have, and made it possible for me to know my heavenly Daddy in a real and more intimate way.

In those early days, I looked to God more as a daddy than as a Father. He held and comforted me. His strength made me able to face the difficulties of life. I found in God a refuge and a fortress, a present help in the time of trouble.

MOVING FROM DADDY'S LAP TO FATHER'S PURPOSE

In You, O Lord, I put my trust; let me never be ashamed; deliver me in Your righteousness. Bow down Your ear to me, deliver me speedily; be my rock of refuge, a fortress of defense to save me. For You are my rock and my fortress; therefore, for Your name's sake, lead me and guide me (Psalm 31:1-3).

These Scriptures describe my walk with God in those days. Yet, God was also dealing with me as a father would his son. Although my heavenly Father was with me to comfort me in my life, as my Father He had also chosen this life for me. The Lord was directing the path of my life in a very specific way. In all my discomfort, God was a comfort. Even though He had the power, He didn't take my distresses from me. He simply comforted me until the point in time when He could change me into the mature person He wanted me to be. The day would come when my Father would wean me from His comforting arms in order to strengthen me for the purpose He had for my life. It was a purpose I could not achieve as a child, always running to my Father for comfort. However, when I became mature, I wouldn't just seek His comfort, but I would seek His strength and wisdom. I wouldn't want Him to simply hide me from the enemy but to teach me how I could defeat my enemies and be an overcomer in this life. I wouldn't want Him just to be something for me; I would want to be something for Him. I wouldn't say, "Daddy, rescue me," but I would say, "Father, your son is ready to be like You." This attitude of the overcomer is the only attitude that will bring our full inheritance! There will always be those moments when we need to run to Daddy's lap for a little encouragement. Those times will never leave us. But we must be prepared to move beyond the place of needing encouragement to the place of being reshaped into His image as a son.

> *He who overcomes shall inherit all things, and I will be his God and he shall be My son* (Revelation 21:7, emphasis added).

To get where He was supposed to be, Jesus started to suffer the day His ministry began. He accepted His life and now He was accepting His purpose. Jesus had to establish Himself in the natural as a son first, before He could step into His spiritual inheritance. Jesus had to come to terms with who He was in the natural before He could receive the full complement of His spiritual calling. The Father had been an overseer in His life until this point; now, the Father's role would be the vital part of His life.

When Jesus came up from the waters of baptism, the Father made a declaration of approval from Heaven over him. The Father's heavenly declaration of approval came after He had walked out His relationship in His *natural*, earthly life. This is a biblical principle.

> *However, the spiritual is not first, but the natural, and afterward the spiritual* (1 Corinthians 15:46).

Many Christians want spiritual blessing without dealing with the "natural" side of life. Jesus was truly God, but also truly man. He came to show us how God would live as a man. Once He had fully experienced His natural life, He was ready to exercise authority in the spiritual. His natural would be the foundation for the spiritual. Before Jesus would be led by the Spirit to the wilderness, God the Father was working compassion in His heart.

TRAINING AS SONS

As a father I have loved my children very much. As they were growing up, I was probably more involved than most fathers. When the children were very young, however, they needed their mother more than me. I jokingly told my wife she could have the kids until they were old enough to talk and walk, then they would be ready for what I could do for them. My wife actually enjoyed the personal care of bathing and tending to the personal needs of the children. I loved calling my wife to assist in these chores. I loved the fact my wife nursed the children because she was the only one who had a bottle when they called in the night. I am so glad I had a wife who loved those things! As much as they loved me, when the children were sick, they called for Mom. The daddy is the mother's helper, but he will never truly be a substitute for Mom.

As a daddy, a father should certainly be a willing helper for his wife. The true fathering role, however, is first a visionary thing. The greatest impact the father has on the children when they are young, besides providing for and protecting them, is the example the children see lived before them. The example the father sets for the sons is of the utmost importance. Jesus claimed this to be the most important influence on His ministry.

Then Jesus answered and said to them, "Most assuredly, I say to you, the Son can do nothing of Himself, but what He sees the Father do; for whatever He does, the Son also does in like manner. For the Father loves the Son, and shows Him all things that He Himself does; and He will show Him greater works than these, that you may marvel" (John 5:19-20).

It is when the children are older that the role of the father takes on a greater role. When they are older, it is time to prepare them for the world and adulthood.

It is at this point that we find the Father in Heaven taking a more visible place with the Son. The Father will now help guide Him through His public ministry on the earth. Not all Christians can be treated like sons because we are not prepared or available. There is a point in our lives, however, when God can say we are ready. At that point, we must recognize our life will no longer be the same. Then, we will see God dealing with us as sons, requiring more responsibility and more intensely preparing us for our destiny. We must be willing to accept this shift and submit ourselves to this training process of the Father. This process will be critical for laying the foundation of all future work on behalf of Father.

If you endure chastening, God deals with you as with sons; for what son is there whom a father does not chasten? But if you

41

are without chastening, of which all have become partakers, then you are illegitimate and not sons (Hebrews 12:7-8).

CRYING OUT TO GOD

I learned this lesson in a very difficult way. In the summer of 1994, I was at a minister's conference with my staff. Because I wasn't feeling well one day, I jokingly told my wife during the evening service, to keep an eye on me if I should "fall out," because it wouldn't be by the Holy Spirit. After the service, in the foyer of the hotel, I had what was later diagnosed as a grand mal seizure. For the next nine months, I had seizure activity almost daily. I was on medication; however, it controlled only the problem; it didn't provide a cure. This was the worst time of my life. I had faced physical infirmity before, but this was much worse. Whether it was the disease or the medication—I am not sure, but my emotions were adversely affected. Sometimes it seemed like I had no feelings at all. This caused me great distress because up to this point, my relationship with God was very "feel" oriented. This brought a severe spiritual conflict. I remember crying out to my heavenly Daddy seeking the comfort I had often depended upon. It seemed like He was a million miles away and was not hearing my prayer.

I kept asking God if there was something I needed to surrender to Him. My spiritual walk was built upon the concept that, when confronted with crisis, one must search his heart and find the things that must be surrendered to God in order to get out of the crisis. With every crisis there was always a lot of "soul-searching." I kept asking, "God, what is it You are asking of me?" The Lord told me in no uncertain terms that He didn't want me to surrender anything to Him; He wanted me to struggle with Him!

This went against the grain of all that I knew and had experienced in the past. It just wasn't in me to do what He was asking of me. I told Him He must not love me like I thought He did, because if He did, He certainly wouldn't allow me to suffer so! He told me that what I was going through was similar to what Jacob endured when he wrestled with the Lord. I would need to struggle through this crisis rather than be delivered from this crisis; but in the end, I would have the blessing of a changed life.

The words of God have always been sweet in my mouth. I love to hear from God. But sometimes His word can be bitter, as it was in this case. This word was not what I wanted to hear, and the process of working that word in me would also be bitter.

> *So I went to the angel and said to him, "Give me the little book." And he said to me, "Take and eat it; and it will make your stomach bitter, but it will be as sweet as honey in your mouth"* (Revelation 10:9).

This was not just a simple word that would make me feel good about my circumstances. This was a word that would work deeply, plowing the very core of my being. My spirit would no longer be able to just cry out to "Abba" or Daddy. I was now growing up and recognizing Him as my Father. When I finally passed this trial, surely, my spirit would cry out "Abba, Father." My spirit would agree with His Spirit that I was a son of God. This new stage of relationship could only come as I was willing to suffer with Him.

> *For you did not receive the spirit of bondage again to fear, but you received the Spirit of adoption by whom we cry out, "Abba, Father." The Spirit Himself bears witness with our spirit that we are children of God, and if children, then heirs—heirs of God and joint heirs with Christ, if indeed we suffer with Him, that we may also be glorified together* (Romans 8:15-17).

In my affliction, as with many of the sons of God, I was refusing to allow myself to grow past the "Abba" stage. I wanted a daddy but did not want a father. The Spirit of God within us wants to cry out "Abba," and also "Father," not just one or the other. As it is in the natural, so it is in the spiritual. Just as the young child will grow and mature and his relationship with his dad will change, so it is with God's people. Don't refuse the new place of relationship God wants to bring you to. Realize that this level of growth will come with a cost, but remember that beyond every cost is a blessing.

43

GIVING UP YOUR CHILDHOOD

As I was growing up, in order for me to experience the responsibilities of adulthood, I had to release the innocence of my childhood. I had to be willing to let myself learn to live in the world of adult men and women. I had to face the challenges as a man. I would certainly still need advice and help, but now I had to embrace the new responsibilities of living in that world. Once the training had been completed, the weight of moving out into the world was upon my shoulders.

It is time for the children of God to see that Father's goal is to prepare them to be sons and daughters. The whole work of God in your life is to prepare you to live and function as adult sons and daughters in the Kingdom. When I become a man, the Word declares, I will put away childish things. I will become *perfected*. This is a scary word for most of the Christian world, but it simply means complete or mature. It means to reach your destiny as a child of God, being fully developed and ready for the Father's work. Preparation for the work of God is not a miracle performed but a process that we endure in order that the nature of Father is worked into our lives.

> *But when that which is perfect has come, then that which is in part will be done away. When I was a child, I spoke as a child, I understood as a child, I thought as a child; but when I became a man, I put away childish things. For now we see in a mirror, dimly, but then face to face. Now I know in part, but then I shall know just as I also am known* (1 Corinthians 13:10-12).

SEEING THE WORLD FROM FATHER'S EYES

The Church has lived too long in the clouded vision produced by our unwillingness to abandon our childhood. As children, we tend to view life from a purely intellectual and fleshly perspective that distorts our vision.

I remember when I was a child, we lived in an apartment that was at the lower level of a hill, and to reach our entry, you had to walk down that hill. As kids, we rode our sleds down that hill in the winter and our makeshift hot rods in the summer. Was I amazed when I went back to that house as an adult and saw that "big hill!" To my surprise, I found no hill at all, only a slight incline!

How different the world is from a child's point of view. When we make the spiritual shift from kids to adults, our perspective of the world around us will change dramatically. How different our view of the world will be when the Church grows to maturity. We've been paralyzed like the children of Israel when they were called out to God at the Jordan River looking over into the Promised Land. They were accustomed to having all their needs taken care of, and they were afraid of the giants. Now God was calling them to cross over and do things they had never done before. Joshua and Caleb were the only ones able to see from Father's perspective because they had shed their slavish mentalities and were true sons.

When we spiritually grow up, we will be able to see like Joshua and Caleb. Our eyes will not be fixed upon the problems, but on our Father and His promises. Like Joshua we will say, "Those aren't giants; they are bread for us to eat!" We live in a time of being surrounded by great giants. Our culture has been infested with a flood of humanistic philosophies; our schools and our families are under assault. The challenges of our time will require true sons of God who have been tested in the fire and who see life from Father's perspective and will give themselves to the battle.

I have written to you, fathers, because you have known Him who is from the beginning. I have written to you, young men, because you are strong, and the word of God abides in you, and you have overcome the wicked one (1 John 2:14).

PUT AWAY CHILDISH THINGS

The strong ones who are no longer children will gladly put away their childish things. What are these childish things the Word is speaking about?

First, as I just discussed, it is our outlook—how we view our life and the world around us. Secondly, it is the willingness to exchange what is in our hands as kids for what Father wants to entrust us with. As children, we played with toys. What are toys? Toys are miniature versions of the real things. Toys are items that you can trust in the hands of a child. Little girls play with dolls, not babies. Little boys play with toy cars, but we don't give them the keys to our real car. It is the Father's desire to give us the keys to the Kingdom and to invest us with spiritual power. The question is, are we willing to pay the price to grow up so that we can handle that power? I hear in my spirit the cry of the prophet, Jeremiah, as he longs to see his people move away from superficial and selfish lifestyles of God's people.

> *Because from the least of them even to the greatest of them, everyone is given to covetousness; and from the prophet even to the priest, everyone deals falsely. They have also healed the hurt of My people slightly, saying, "Peace, peace!" when there is no peace* (Jeremiah 6:13-14, emphasis added).

Paul puts it a different way in First Corinthians 13 declaring that when we emerge into adulthood, we automatically put away childish things. For grown adults to hold on to childish things is an indication of a spiritual disorder.

> *For we know in part and we prophesy in part. But when that which is perfect has come, then that which is in part will be done away. When I was a child, I spoke as a child, I understood as a child, I thought as a child; but when I became a man, I put away childish things* (1 Corinthians 13:9-11).

It is so important in this time that we embrace every experience of life that will enable us to move on to perfection and maturity. It will cost us something. You have heard of growing pains? Well, growing up is hard to do. You will suffer as you shed your childhood, but it will be worth the discomfort. This suffering or discomfort will lead you to the glory of God the Father and bring you into a greater place of influence in His world.

As I struggled with these truths, I was finally ready to embrace this hour of affliction knowing that God was taking me to a new level of spiritual maturity. Finally, in May of 1995, after suffering nine months with seizures, the Lord came to me. I was in prayer when the Lord spoke to me from Isaiah 49:

> *Thus saith the Lord, In an acceptable time have I heard thee, and in a day of salvation have I helped thee: and I will preserve thee, and give thee for a covenant of the people, to establish the earth, to cause to inherit the desolate heritages* (Isaiah 49:8 KJV).

That day I was healed. Within a month, I had weaned myself from all the medication and, with the doctor's consultation, began a new drug-free life with no seizures! Thank You, Father.

I also found in this chapter of Isaiah, as a treasure hidden in a field, the reason for the pain I had endured. The Father actually wanted to enlarge me. This calamity was not to my harm, but to my glory. God wasn't trying to tear me down, but to build me up. As a result of walking through this ordeal, the purposes of God had come to a fuller expression in my life. During those days, I thought that my whole Christian experience had been in vain. Despondently, I contemplated, *I have served the Lord from my mother's womb and this is my reward?* It didn't seem quite fair. I could not see God's ultimate purposes in this physical trial.

But God assured me during those days that my reward would indeed come; but first, God was going to work something in me that would expand my abilities. My earlier relationship with God had not been in vain! The life I had been living was just one phase of my relationship with Father. However, this affliction was creating a foundation for something bigger. It was bigger than me, and that is why I didn't want it. But God stretched me during those days so that I could harmonize with His purposes. My Father empowered me, and now I say, thank You, Father.

> *"Then I said, 'I have labored in vain, I have spent my strength for nothing and in vain; yet surely my just reward is with the Lord, and my work with my God.'" "And now the Lord says, who formed Me from the womb to be His Servant, to bring Jacob back to Him, so that Israel is gathered to Him (for I shall be glorious in the eyes of the Lord, and My God shall be My strength), indeed He says, 'It is too small a thing that You*

47

should be My Servant to raise up the tribes of Jacob, and to restore the preserved ones of Israel; I will also give You as a light to the Gentiles, that You should be My salvation to the ends of the earth' " (Isaiah 49:4-6).

My submission to the call of being a son of God opened the door for the biggest miracle in my life. God eventually did something *for* me, but first He did something *in* me. This is the pattern for bringing the sons of God into maturity.

Now to Him who is able to do exceedingly abundantly above all that we ask or think, according to the power that works in us (Ephesians 3:20).

Have you noticed a change in your relationship with God? Is something different? Are you yearning for a past experience or longing for the "good ole days," but not finding them?

If you will stop and take time to listen, you just might hear Him say that it's not time to look back to your past, but to look forward to your destiny. It is not the time for fantasizing about yesterday's experience. God has a new experience to prepare you for a new day!

Chapter Four

Dealing With the Devil in Your Garden

Then Jesus was led up by the Spirit into the wilderness to be tempted by the devil (Matthew 4:1).

In Jesus, the Father has a true Son. This Son would grow up and become more than just a child of the Father. He would become a young man who would face the problems of life as an overcomer. The Son would reflect the nature of His Father in the world of man. He would have to be willing to accept the responsibility of the Father's Kingdom that had been entrusted to Him. There was a destiny on His life, given by the Father, and He would have to be willing to abandon His own will and desires to live a life for Himself. In the end, He would destroy the power the devil had been given by the abdication of the first son of God, Adam, and then He would reestablish Father's Kingdom.

He who sins is of the devil, for the devil has sinned from the beginning. For this purpose the Son of God was manifested, that He might destroy the works of the devil (1 John 3:8).

FACING DOWN THE ENEMY

After the Father affirmed His approval of Jesus at the river Jordan, He was led by the Spirit into the desert to be tempted by the devil. The timing was not a mere coincidence. The Father had an approved Son ready for the next phase of His life. Now, He would stand in the place that the first son, Adam, stood in. When the Lord God created Adam, He put him in the Garden of Eden to dress and to keep it. This son, Adam, was created for a specific purpose. His purpose was to have an intimate relationship with his Father, and from the power of that relationship he was destined to take dominion of God's creation. This dominion would be manifested in his faithfulness as a steward over the garden God had placed him in. Adam was given the privilege of "full use" of the garden for his pleasure, except for that one little tree that was in the middle of the garden. This tree was the tree of the knowledge of good and evil.

As long as Adam was faithful to his stewardship by guarding and keeping what God had put in his hands, he not only could enjoy the blessings of the garden, but he also had access to the tree of life. The name *Eden* means "delightful living." From the beginning, God has wanted us to not only have life, but also to have it more abundantly! The pathway to experiencing this abundance was the same for Adam as it is for us—by obedience to our Father and remaining faithful to the stewardship of His domain.

In fulfilling this responsibility, man would have to contend with his own desire, but also he would have to contend with satan. *Satan*, meaning "adversary," is also called the devil, which means accuser. Both the first Adam and the second Adam had to face this adversary head-on. One would fail, and the other would succeed

Jesus had to go to a desert. The first Adam was surrounded by a garden of delicious fruit trees; the second Adam would be in a desert without food. Their environments in which they faced their enemy were in total contrast. However, they had something in common—in both locations there existed an adversary.

DEALING WITH THE DEVIL IN YOUR GARDEN

Why does there have to be a devil? More importantly, why is there a devil in our garden? Why does there have to be a fly in every ointment?

Most Christians believe the devil is a "leftover" from another time, another place—that just happens to be in our world. They see the devil simply as a tragedy from a pre-adamic time. The Scriptures indicate that the devil had a special place in Heaven's realm before Father's throne, but because of sin he was cast out of Heaven. Now he lives in the earth to cause havoc for us and mess up Father's plan.

If this is all true, we cannot assume he is on the planet earth by coincidence or divine oversight. When we think that way, we fail to see the sovereignty and power of Almighty God. We must see satan as a part of God's plan in some way. God has a reason for allowing him to be here. Father always has a unique way of turning tragedy into triumph, fitting all things into His divine purposes. God uses both good and evil to fulfill His plans.

> *That they may know from the rising of the sun to its setting that there is none besides Me. I am the Lord, and there is no other; I form the light and create darkness, I make peace and create calamity; I, the Lord, do all these things* (Isaiah 45:6-7).

Once we see the devil as part of the program, we can deal with the problem accordingly. You see, the devil is a part of God's plan. It is not so important to know where he came from as to know what purpose he serves in hindering God's intention for His sons. The mature son of God understands he must be an overcomer in all things. The issue is not the obstacle to overcome, but how we overcome. A mother would never allow a devil in the playhouse, but a father understands that there will always be one in the schoolhouse. He trains his sons, not to run from the bully, but to stand and face him. This is how we train our sons to be men and not just children. Once we understand there is a purpose behind the problem, we can stand with confidence knowing that as we stand in relationship with Jesus, we will be able to succeed in our resistance of the enemy. We will realize the problem is not without; it is within.

> *You are of God, little children, and have overcome them, because He who is in you is greater than he who is in the world* (1 John 4:4).

FACING THE WORLD WITHIN YOU

Amazingly enough, Adam and Jesus faced the same temptations. The world has changed, but the Word declares there is nothing new under the sun. Our world is more technologically advanced, and we are blessed with many things that make our life easier than those of previous generations. But, in spite of the many advances, man still struggles with the same issues of the heart. The outer world has taken on a new appearance, but the inner world remains the same. God has told us, like Jesus, we must overcome the world and he that is in the world. When the Word speaks of the world, it is referring to three things:

> *Do not love the world or the things in the world. If anyone loves the world, the love of the Father is not in him. For all that is in the world—the lust of the flesh, the lust of the eyes, and the pride of life—is not of the Father but is of the world. And the world is passing away, and the lust of it; but he who does the will of God abides forever* (1 John 2:15-17).

The world consists of the lust of the flesh, the lust of the eyes, and the pride of life. Interestingly enough, this is the same technique that the devil used on Adam in the garden.

> *So when the woman saw that the tree was good for food, that it was pleasant to the eyes, and a tree desirable to make one wise, she took of its fruit and ate. She also gave to her husband with her, and he ate. Then the eyes of both of them were opened, and they knew that they were naked; and they sewed fig leaves together and made themselves coverings* (Genesis 3:6-7).

The problem that Adam and Eve faced, and the problem Jesus faced, is the same problem that we face as we prepare ourselves to become the sons of God and serve His purposes in our generation. The issue really isn't the devil at all. If our heart is right with God, the devil has no power over us. This is what Jesus told the disciples as He was getting ready to face the cross:

> *I will no longer talk much with you, for the ruler of this world is coming, and he has nothing in Me* (John 14:30).

WHEN THERE IS NOTHING IN US, THERE CAN BE NOTHING AGAINST US

The devil will seek to make war with us, but he has no real authority over us. The devious tactics he uses against us, rather than pull us down, simply become a test of our own faith and serve to strengthen our position in God.

"No weapon formed against you shall prosper, and every tongue which rises against you in judgment you shall condemn. This is the heritage of the servants of the Lord, and their righteousness is from Me," says the Lord (Isaiah 54:17).

God, our Father, doesn't just promise to protect us; He promises to take the bad and use it for good. The plans the devil has devised to destroy you will only bring you to a higher place in God. This is what the Bible says concerning the cross. Because the rulers of this world did not know what God was doing, they became unwilling accomplices to the purpose of God. These religious leaders thought they were stopping Jesus, but they were only creating a pathway that would lead Him to glory and the fulfillment of His Father's plans.

But we speak the wisdom of God in a mystery, the hidden wisdom which God ordained before the ages for our glory, which none of the rulers of this age knew; for had they known, they would not have crucified the Lord of glory. But as it is written: "Eye has not seen, nor ear heard, nor have entered into the heart of man the things which God has prepared for those who love Him" (1 Corinthians 2:7-9).

God is leading us to glory! It is our destiny. No one can stop what God wants to do in your life. They can only help it along. God will turn the tables on everything in your life to accomplish His purpose for you!

And we know that all things work together for good to those who love God, to those who are the called according to His purpose. For whom He foreknew, He also predestined to be conformed to the image of His Son, that He might be the firstborn among many brethren. Moreover whom He predestined, these He also called; whom He called, these He also justified; and whom He justified, these He also glorified. What then shall we say to these things? If God is for us, who can be against us? (Romans 8:28-31)

WHAT MUST WE DO?

Therefore submit to God. Resist the devil and he will flee from you. Draw near to God and He will draw near to you. Cleanse your hands, you sinners; and purify your hearts, you double-minded (James 4:7-8).

The trials of our life are for our learning and purification. The wilderness has a purpose for your life.

And you shall remember that the Lord your God led you all the way these forty years in the wilderness, to humble you and test you, to know what was in your heart, whether you would keep His commandments or not. So He humbled you, allowed you to hunger, and fed you with manna which you did not know nor did your fathers know, that He might make you know that man shall not live by bread alone; but man lives by every word that proceeds from the mouth of the Lord (Deuteronomy 8:2-3).

When we go through our testing and when the attitudes of our heart become manifest, then we can take the opportunity of evaluating our inward motivations. We then simply allow ourselves to come under the surgical knife of Father, and as He cuts, He can remove what hinders us and heal what hurts us. In the end, it is Father's desire that we might be able to stand before Him fully representing His image and prepared to fulfill His purposes.

THE FIRST TEST

The first test Jesus faced was similar to the first test faced by the children of Israel in the wilderness. It was the test of the lust of the flesh. Lust of the flesh can manifest itself in many ways; but for Adam and Eve, the children of Israel, and even for our Lord, it centered on satisfying one's ravenous hunger. When the children of Israel were hungry, they cried out in agony pleading for food to relieve the pangs of hunger. God responded to their plea and fed them with the bread from Heaven. They didn't realize that this test was not about how long they could go without food; it was about faith, about trusting Father in the midst of dark circumstances. Could they trust God to take care of them in the midst of this trial?

When the Lord sent the bread from Heaven, the children of Israel looked at it and said, "What's that?" which is what the word *manna* really means. Even the Lord's provision became a mystery to them. Sometimes God's solutions are more puzzling than the problem we are confronting. His answer did not seem like a solution. So why did God send the manna? God wanted them to continue to walk by faith, even in the manner in which He answered their cry. He wanted them to see the preciousness of seeking and hearing the Word of God for themselves. For God, the absence of bread created an opportunity for His people to enter into a new level of fellowship with Him. But for them, it was cruel and unnecessary, and they could not see beyond the test nor focus on the spiritual opportunity that the test had provided. Oh, how different things look from Heaven than they do from earth.

This example from the history of Israel also provides us with an illustration of how the Father desires to bring forth mature sons in the earth. When the children of Israel asked for bread, God didn't give them bread; *He gave them something to make into bread.* This demonstrates the difference between the ministry of the Daddy and the ministry of the Father. When young children cry out, we quickly respond to their cries with a quick resolution and comfort. There eventually comes a time, however, when as parents we need to let the children take care of some things themselves. In Egypt, God did everything for the children of Israel. In the wilderness, He was trying to get them to take a role in the process. When taking the children of Israel out of Egypt, God did all the work. They even resisted the process, but God still brought them out with a mighty hand. In the wilderness, God wanted them to exercise faith and participate in the process. This would prepare them for the Promised Land where they would have to work the land for their provision. It wouldn't be all God. God would supply the ingredients; they would make the bread.

Oftentimes, we think God is not answering our prayers because He doesn't deliver ready-made. Don't miss the Father's provision. It might just be ingredients; but it will feed you, if you believe it to be God's provision for you. The first son, Adam, was not given a grocery store; he was given a garden. This is the pattern God has for His sons.

You will notice how Jesus, in contrast to Adam and the children of Israel, answered this scheming temptation with the Word:

But He answered and said, "It is written, 'Man shall not live by bread alone, but by every word that proceeds from the mouth of God'" (Matthew 4:4).

Many people take these verses and declare, "See, the way to fight the devil is with the Word." The problem, as you can see, is that the devil knows the Word better than most Christians. Jesus won this battle, not because He had a Scripture for the devil, but because He was not using a Bible verse as some kind of magic. He was responding from His heart and love for His Father. The devil can win arguments, but he cannot defeat a pure heart. Passion will always triumph over any argument. Adam and Eve had the best Father could have offered. He had created a beautiful world for them, and He walked with them in that wonderful world, expressing His love for them. Adam and Eve had enjoyed the Father's presence as they listened to His powerful word. Unfortunately, they were foolish enough to believe there could be something better than the favor of Father. Too bad they didn't understand their error in judgment until it was too late.

THE SECOND TEST

The second temptation Jesus faced was the pride of life. The devil wanted Jesus to walk in the sin of presumption, which is always rooted in pride.

Pride goes before destruction, and a haughty spirit before a fall. Better to be of a humble spirit with the lowly, than to divide the spoil with the proud (Proverbs 16:18-19).

Again, the battle wasn't won because Jesus was the Bible-answer man. Jesus had the humble heart that destroys the devil every time. The Church has yet to learn the power of a humble heart. Our pursuit for power, position, and recognition will doom us every time.

But He gives more grace. Therefore He says: "God resists the proud, but gives grace to the humble." Therefore submit to God. Resist the devil and he will flee from you (James 4:6-7).

The proud heart is always telling God what to do. Imagine! Do we really think we're smart enough to tell God what to do? In essence, that is exactly what we are doing when we put God to the test. We are saying that if you want to do the right thing, you follow directions from me. The devil has a real playground in the person's life who trusts in his own ingenuity and influence.

The person of the humble heart looks at his life and says, "Look what the Lord has done!" He understands that God's power is best demonstrated through weakness. He can see that left to himself, his life could have been ruined or unfulfilled and drifting without purpose. Adam and Eve thought life would be so much better under their control. All they had to do was eat from the tree, and then they would have the wisdom to make their own choices rather than just rely on God. Again, they didn't get the message until it was too late. Don't be rebellious! Listen! And the Lord will surely speak concerning your life, giving you direction, help, and protection all along the way.

Therefore, as the Holy Spirit says: "Today, if you will hear His voice, do not harden your hearts as in the rebellion, in the day of trial in the wilderness, where your fathers tested Me, tried Me, and saw My works forty years" (Hebrews 3:7-9).

It is clear that Adam and Eve had been given a very special gift from God. The gift God gave was the gift of choice. No other creature had that gift—the gift of self-determination. This gift from Father gives us a clue as to the devil's purpose in God's world. How could we say we have choice if no alternative is given? The Lord not only provided a choice, but He also provided an agitator for the other side. If God wanted to exercise authoritarian control, He wouldn't have allowed for opposition and certainly not an advocate to promote the opposing view. But God was creating a world that would be full of choices that would not only require difficult decisions, but in the process, would also teach us discernment and judgment. These are two necessary qualities, discernment and judgment, in the life of a mature person. What an awesome position God has desired for us from the beginning! *We think He is looking to enslave us, when in fact He is looking to empower us!* The first couple was seeking independence and instead found slavery. God is not looking for slaves, but people who will be in relationship with Him as sons, knowing how to trust the Father in the difficult decisions of life.

Human relationships, from a godly point of view, are not about bondage; they are about interdependence. When we think of relationships only in terms of independence for ourselves, then we often look at those relationships as a means of bringing people into dependence upon us. True independence for many people requires that they are able to control those around them. Many humans are inclined to reduce relationships to a form of subservience and self-promotion. When a person grows to a place of greater maturity, he should not be looking for the time when he will be independent from others, but rather how he can take his proper place of interdependence among others. Life is about relationships. It is not only about freedom; it is about serving. True liberty requires both. Jesus made it very clear that the Kingdom leadership model was based upon servanthood. Paul then amplified this point by saying the whole body functions on the basis of serving one another.

> *For even the Son of Man did not come to be served, but to serve, and to give His life a ransom for many* (Mark 10:45).

> *Submitting to one another in the fear of God (Ephesians 5:21).*

God has not chosen you to be independent of other people, and neither has He called you to be in bondage to others. God wants a relationship of interdependence between those in His great family. You cannot take His place as Father, and He does not want to take your place in manifesting His life to others. God wants us to be in partnership with Him. How amazing! Once we understand God is not a taskmaster but a Father, we can join ourselves in a real partnership with God. Adam was far from a slave in the day of his creation. He was given a place of authority and dominion. Eve stood right along with him as a joint heir also having authority and responsibility. They were given a position of dominion over "the garden," and God never tried to usurp their authority. Neither did He want them to usurp His. Much rebellion in the local church arises from people being controlled by leadership and not understanding their place of authority and responsibility. In this day, the Church must move to a higher level of understanding in the ultimate purposes of God.

THE FINAL TEST

Finally, Jesus faced the last of His temptations—the lust of the eye. The devil gave Him a quick showcase of all the kingdoms of the world, and in closing, made Him a deal he thought that Jesus could not refuse. "Worship me and I will give you all these things," the devil proudly declared. The word *worship* is associated with the word *worth*. God is worthy of our praise and adoration. He is worthy of our sacrifice. When we are in the high places of worship, it is easy to sing of His great worth. But when our eyes begin to stray to all of the "things" around us, we become distracted with their worldly worth. We look and see what someone else has, and we want it. Although Adam and Eve had no one to compare themselves to, they were tempted to compare themselves to God. The devil said, "You could be like God." To Jesus he said, "You could be like me." Sadly, most of us are living our lives comparing ourselves to others and wanting to be like them. This is probably the most trying test for parents and their kids. The kids are always comparing themselves to one another. It is called sibling rivalry, and there is a lot of sibling rivalry in God's family— always wishing we had what another has. In this environment, the devil has a lot of room for maneuvering and manipulating God's people. There is always someone or something he can get our eyes focused on.

The sad thing about these kinds of family conflicts is that our uniqueness as an individual is often overlooked or minimized. We disregard the great gifts that Father has given us and the value He has placed on our lives. In the created world around us, the most valuable is the most precious or rare. How sad it is when we strive to be like others. In our striving, we then rob the world of the blessing of our uniqueness.

I remember when my wife became pregnant with our second child. I was as excited about the second child as I had been with the first. Then one day I started to worry. Because I loved my first child so much, how could I ever love another one as much as the first? The greatness of my love for my son didn't seem to leave much room for more love. I actually prayed about this, and the Lord spoke to me. He said, "You will love the second as much as you love the first. But you will love them differently. Each child is unique, and each will have a unique relationship with you." These words are also true regarding your heavenly Father's love for you. We are so concerned about everyone else that we fail to see the beauty of what God is doing in our own lives.

Jesus knew who He was and who His Father was. Because of that, He had the heart of a true worshiper, and the devil has no power over the true worshiper.

THE FATHER'S TIMING AND HIS WAYS ARE ALWAYS PERFECT

Did you notice that the devil began each of his temptations with, "If You are the Son of God..."? As soon as the Father declared Him to be the Son, the devil was out to challenge Him. You can't make it through the wilderness without knowing who you are. When you know who you are, you don't have to compare yourself with others, and you don't have to compete with them either. Knowing and accepting your identity will resolve so many issues of shame, insecurity, and striving in your life.

This was the problem with the children of Israel in the desert. They always had their eye looking back to Egypt. They didn't know they were the "head" and not the "tail," and that Father was transforming them and delivering them from a slave mentality. Before they could go into the Promised Land, however, they had to roll off the reproach of Egypt. They had to get rid of the attitude cast upon

them by the Egyptians when they were in slavery. Joshua had to cir-
cumcise them again at the hill of foreskins to prepare them to go into
the Promised Land. I believe our "Joshua," Jesus Christ, wants to roll
off of us our reproach in this day so we can go into the promised land
of our destiny.

Notice once more the crafty deception that the serpent used
against Jesus. He wasn't offering Jesus something that He wasn't
allowed to have. The trap set by satan was in the timing and the
method. He was offering the kingdoms of this world ahead of time
and in a different process than laid out by His Father. Here is a great
key for all who would be His sons. In order to experience Father's
favor, you must wait on His timing and be prepared to accomplish
His will through the pathway that He has designed for you.
Remember that shortcuts lead to dead ends.

Jesus was born to be an heir of the kingdoms of this world. It
just wasn't the right time nor the appropriate way. Jesus, as the Son
of God, simply had to be patient and faithful, and all these things
would eventually be His. The sons of God in the earth must be careful not to allow what we see around us to cause us to run ahead of
God. We must learn to be a partner in our work with Him as we seek
to take possession of the Kingdom.

The son of God realizes the timing of the Father is perfect and
that the ways of the Lord are right. A blessing out of season could
result in a curse. (Consider Adam and Eve.) As Jesus rode through
Jerusalem, listening to the praise of the people, He faced the opportunity to let the people crown Him ahead of time. If He had allowed
Himself to be persuaded by the people, they would have made Him
King out of season and in the wrong way.

In the end, the devil had actually assisted in training Jesus,
when Jesus settled early on that He must always walk in the Father's
way and the Father's timing.

*Therefore when Jesus perceived that they were about to come
and take Him by force to make Him king, He departed again to
the mountain by Himself alone* (John 6:15).

Remember Jesus said:

But seek the kingdom of God, and all these things shall be added to you. Do not fear, little flock, for it is your Father's good pleasure to give you the kingdom (Luke 12:31-32).

This is the day for the unveiling of the sons of God. All of creation is on tiptoes as they await that moment. What Jesus accomplished in 40 days God's people often spend a whole lifetime trying to fulfill. It is the timing of God for us to go on to the greater things in the Kingdom. It is possible to overcome the world and the devil. Jesus accomplished it in the garden; we can accomplish this as well.

The world that we are called to overcome is the system or order created from man's rebellion against God. We must overcome and transcend that world. We need to respond to a higher level of faith. How? We need the faith of the overcomer.

For whatever is born of God overcomes the world. And this is the victory that has overcome the world—our faith (1 John 5:4).

With this faith, we can experience the Father's favor and discover the source of the power to overcome. It does not originate in our strength, but in Christ within us. This will lead us to victory.

You are of God, little children, and have overcome them, because He who is in you is greater than he who is in the world (1 John 4:4).

Chapter Five

Do You Really Know Who You Are?

Jesus, knowing that the Father had given all things into His hands, and that He had come from God and was going to God, rose from supper and laid aside His garments, took a towel and girded Himself (John 13:3-4).

In the wilderness temptation, Jesus had a face-off with the devil. And Jesus won! As He resisted the devil at every turn, the devil eventually had to flee. Jesus set a pattern for us so that we will triumph over the devil every time. Jesus also established a very important principle concerning His own identity. Remember that the devil's temptations were prefaced by his insidious attack made by this statement, "If You are the Son of God...." Jesus was not lured into this trap because He did not have an identity problem. If He had had one, He would have been an easy prey for the devourer. A person with an identity problem will always be seeking approval and trying to prove himself to others in overt and insecure ways. This insecurity about oneself makes him susceptible to anxiety on one hand and flaunting himself on the other. It makes it difficult to simply allow himself to be led by Father's hand.

The Spirit of God cannot lead us if we are living our lives always in reaction to life's circumstances. It will be difficult to sense the Spirit's direction when our own human spirit is crying out for personal expression and attention. An insecure person will be caught in the trap of trying to prove something, rather than be what he was designed to be. In the act of proving oneself, a person is rendered ineffective in establishing their identity in God. —

Jesus knew who He was. He knew who He was as a person, because He knew who He was in the Father. He saw His life and identity flowing out of His relationship with His Father.

Then Jesus answered and said to them, "Most assuredly, I say to you, the Son can do nothing of Himself, but what He sees the Father do; for whatever He does, the Son also does in like manner (John 5:19).

CHOSEN BY THE FATHER

When we come to God, we must see that our reconciliation to God also includes our reconciliation to our eternal destiny. Jesus knew where He came from—He came from God. Because Jesus knew where He came from, He also knew where He was going. He was going back to the Father after fulfilling His earthly destiny. What a wonderful day it will be for the Church when we realize where we came from. When we see our beginning in God, we will see ourselves in a whole new light. You did not choose God; He chose you. You are not born of the will of man, but of the will of God. You are not just an accident no matter the circumstances of your birth. You are not simply the result of the planning of two people who decided to have a baby. You are chosen by God!

Just as He chose us in Him before the foundation of the world, that we should be holy and without blame before Him in love, having predestined us to adoption as sons by Jesus Christ to Himself, according to the good pleasure of His will (Ephesians 1:4-5).

Not only were you chosen of God, you were created by the works of His hands.

"Yet hear now, O Jacob My servant, and Israel whom I have chosen. Thus says the Lord who made you and formed you from the womb, who will help you: 'Fear not, O Jacob My servant; and you, Jeshurun, whom I have chosen'"(Isaiah 44:1-2).

You should not be in a quandary as to your identity nor be in a struggle trying to prove who you are. You are a child of God, and He has created you uniquely for His purpose. Because you are created for His purpose, you should not be struggling with your identity, or your destiny, or your abilities to fulfill that calling. You should be reconciling with Father so that you can find and accept the purpose for which you were created.

> *Woe to him who strives with his Maker! Let the potsherd strive with the potsherds of the earth! Shall the clay say to him who forms it, "What are you making?" Or shall your handiwork say, "He has no hands"? Woe to him who says to his father, "What are you begetting?" Or to the woman, "What have you brought forth?"* (Isaiah 45:9-10)

A LIFE THAT REFLECTS THE GLORY

When the Church settles the issue of who they are, the world will begin to see what the Church really is. This will result in a great harvest and blessing. The world will begin to see the most important part of us—the reflection of Christ in us. Empowered by the security that comes from an assured identity as the sons of God, we will be able to more clearly reveal the glory of God to our generation. The world will be drawn to the light created by that reflection, and great power of God will shine forth from us!

> *Thus says the Lord: "The labor of Egypt and merchandise of Cush and of the Sabeans, men of stature, shall come over to you, and they shall be yours; they shall walk behind you, they shall come over in chains; and they shall bow down to you. They will make supplication to you, saying, 'Surely God is in you, and there is no other; there is no other God'"* (Isaiah 45:14).

When Jesus Christ, the firstborn Son, came into the world, He came to reveal the glory of the Father. The glory of God is not what He does, but who He is. When Moses asked to see the glory, these are the words he heard as he was hidden in the mountain:

> *And the Lord passed before him and proclaimed, "The Lord, the Lord God, merciful and gracious, longsuffering, and abounding in goodness and truth"* (Exodus 34:6).

God's glory is reflected in His compassion and grace towards the sons of men. When we think of purpose, our thoughts turn towards different actions or works that will bring glory to God. The simple fact is, we have all been called to the same purpose. Our purpose is to reveal the glory of who God is to our generation—to reflect His compassion in a world eaten up with rejection. We will demonstrate that glorious purpose in many different ways.

If we don't discover the main purpose of our destiny, then we will struggle with life at every turn. Not only will we struggle with life, but we will also struggle with one another. Jesus did not have these struggles, because He knew where He came from and where He was going. He didn't even struggle when confronted by Pilate before He went to the cross. Why? Because Jesus knew life had a purpose, and He was going to fulfill His purpose, even if it meant death.

> Jesus answered, "My kingdom is not of this world. If My kingdom were of this world, My servants would fight, so that I should not be delivered to the Jews; but now My kingdom is not from here." Pilate therefore said to Him, "Are You a king then?" Jesus answered, "You say rightly that I am a king. For this cause I was born, and for this cause I have come into the world, that I should bear witness to the truth. Everyone who is of the truth hears My voice" (John 18:36-37).

POSITIONING YOURSELF IN GOD'S PURPOSES

Once a person understands that his destiny and purpose is centered in the glory of God rather than personal glory, then he will be able to settle two important conflicts of life. The first conflict is trying to position oneself to fulfill the plans and purpose of God. Many people struggle with how they will or can fulfill the purpose of God for their life. This struggle to fulfill destiny arises out of an improper mind-set. This mind-set is steeped in our heart's desire to fulfill the purpose of God for our benefit.

If you have created a plan to do something for God, chances are it is your plan, not God's. It is most likely born from your human heart's desire. It might even be a notable plan, but it's just not God's plan. Our heart's desires are often contrary to God's desire. We begin with a heart to serve God, but then the human heart creates a plan to satisfy that desire (just look at Abraham). We assume God is behind these plans, without questioning our own motives. The end result is a plan that gets in the way of God's ultimate plan for our life.

YOUR HEART AND THE PLAN OF GOD

A man's heart plans his way, but the Lord directs his steps (Proverbs 16:9).

A man's steps are of the Lord; how then can a man understand his own way? (Proverbs 20:24)

The Word declares that the problem with the human heart is that it is deceitfully wicked and we cannot understand it. We should not walk with God while we are relying on the honesty of our heart to direct us. We should be a people who walk by faith and trust in God. This means we place no confidence in our own ability to bring about God's purposes. We place our confidence in God. This means we believe He will direct our steps even when we cannot see with our human understanding. If you are seeking God's will, He promises to direct your path. It is as simple as that, if you have faith enough to believe it.

Trust in the Lord with all your heart, and lean not on your own understanding; in all your ways acknowledge Him, and He shall direct your paths (Proverbs 3:5-6).

When we first come to the Lord, we can usually document the fact that God accomplished our deliverance, and not us. For me, however, I had to learn that principle later in life. I came to the Lord as a child. It seemed so natural to follow God, especially since I was raised in church. It would have been easy to think that the decisions I made were my choice rather than God's. Yet, when I see the dynamics of my life in comparison to others, I see clearly how my life could have gone in another direction. Through my own experiences and other encounters with God, I can document how God used circumstances I didn't know He was using to bring me to the place He wanted me to be. This all happened without my knowledge.

WHAT GOD STARTS HE WILL FINISH

When I was 17 years old, I had the typical desires of a young man. I wanted a girlfriend. One girl I especially liked told me she couldn't like me as a boyfriend because I was such a "good friend." Shoot me or hate me, but don't tell me you don't see me as a guy you would want as a boyfriend. I complained to God about this matter. I felt the least He could do was give me a girlfriend, since I was such a good Christian. I wanted a girlfriend, and at that time, that was the greatest motivation in my life.

One day, a very good-looking girl invited me to a place called The Prayer House. This was during the Jesus People movement, and many young people were flocking to the move of God. But I wasn't thinking about prayer at all when I said yes. When we went to the coffee house, I was thrilled. It wasn't the move of God that excited me, but the multitudes of good-looking girls. I had noticed one girl in particular; however, she had a boyfriend there. At testimony time, as everyone was trying to outdo each other with the shock value of their personal experience, this girl's friend confessed that he had been delivered from homosexual sin. I could tell by the look on her face that this was the first time she had heard this story, and she wasn't real pleased. In my own carnal way, I took advantage of the moment by telling her how great it was that her friend had been "delivered" from this sin. It wasn't long before she was unattached and available, and I was rejoicing in my good fortune. As time went on, I discovered there were a lot of unattached, available girls. God had answered my prayer so richly that I thought it was the prophecy of Isaiah being fulfilled when he said, "Seven women will lay hold of one man." God is good! Smile!

Yet, in the midst of my carnal journey, the Father was at work to bring me closer to Him. I was at the *right* place for the *wrong* reason. In one of the services, someone asked if anyone wanted the baptism of the Holy Spirit. I said yes, and as I went forward, all I could think was, *What will the girls think if I don't receive the Holy Spirit?* In the midst of my self-centered behavior, I had a wonderful encounter with the Holy Spirit. God used even my carnal motivations to bring me into a closer walk with Him.

You see, God is really the one who directs our steps even when we appear to be going the wrong way. All God asks of us is that we trust in Him and acknowledge Him, and He will take care of the rest. The goal of our walk of faith should be to begin in the Spirit and also to end in the Spirit. To do this, we must be able to confidently ask ourselves the question, "If the Lord starts the work, shouldn't He be able to finish it?" You see, if God can do so much when we don't even know what is happening, shouldn't we be all the more confident when we become informed participants? What God starts He will finish.

Being confident of this very thing, that He who has begun a good work in you will complete it until the day of Jesus Christ (Philippians 1:6).

CONVERTING EVIL INTO GOOD TO MAKE A BEAUTIFUL LIFE

The second biggest conflict we face is how to deal with our overconfidence in our own ability to perform the task God is asking of us. We must realize that God was at work in our life before we even consented for Him to be. We must also recognize He was at work designing our life before we even existed. We are a wonderful creation brought forth from the power of a loving Father. He chose us. He created us in a special way to be the person He wants us to be. The Scriptures teach us that God uses both the genetic compositions of our life and the environmental influences in our life, to make us into the person He wants us to be.

But now, thus says the Lord, who created you, O Jacob, and He who formed you, O Israel: "Fear not, for I have redeemed you; I have called you by your name; you are Mine" (Isaiah 43:1).

Just think, I am the product of the caring hand of a Father who chose me for His purpose in the beginning of time. Understanding this, we might be tempted to blame God for the difficult circumstances of our life rather than rejoice in His personal oversight over

DISCOVERING FAVOR WITH GOD

our life. The problem with this critical view is that it is a limited view. We cannot see the end from the beginning. We cannot see how God uses difficult circumstances in creating and forming us. Because we cannot see these things, we might be tempted to blame God for the unpleasant experiences in our life and resent Him because we feel abandoned. The important thing to note in this verse is that God redeems our life from destruction. God does not *cause* the evil of our lives; He *uses* the evil.

The word *redeem* means that He buys our life, rescuing us from our slavery. Because He purchased us with His own blood, we belong to Him. He also converts bad things, transforming them into good. It is true God could intervene in history and make everyone of us into His pawns. But the truth is, He isn't looking for pawns; He is looking for sons. He could have controlled the actions of mankind from the beginning; however, if you read clearly, you will see that the Bible makes it clear that God is looking for mankind to be His agents of dominion and to do His work, based upon a free and loving relationship. Don't fight with how things could be. Accept the fact that whatever comes into your life contains the possibility of being reshaped into some kind of beauty in your life. God is not a controlling God, and He has not called us to be controlling sons either. It is time to settle our internal conflicts so we can move forward to fulfill the Father's purpose in our life. As Jesus Christ, the firstborn Son, had to go through chosen circumstances, in a chosen body, with a chosen family; certainly, we must do the same.

THE SECOND FALL

In chapter 4 of the Book of Genesis, we read the story of Cain and Abel. I call this the second fall. Because of the choices that Adam and Eve made in the garden, they abdicated the divine stewardship of the earth and attempted to trade it for God's place in Heaven. The power of the flesh provoked mankind to rebel against the heavenly mandated order. This disorder between Heaven and earth brought disorder to the whole earth. That is why, even in this day, the whole of creation groans for the revealing of the sons of God on the earth. The matrix of God's beautifully created universe was injected with a virus of self-will that created disorder in the system. This vertical breakdown provoked a horizontal breakdown as well. Mankind, out of sync with Heaven, will certainly become at variance with one another. The conflict with God will always result in conflict with man. Why is this true? *If you don't know who you are with God, you will always be in conflict with who you are with man!* In our hearts, we will easily believe our problems are the result of other people in our lives. "If it weren't for the people around us, our life would be perfect." This was the error of Cain.

One day he brought a sacrifice to God, as did his brother Abel. God accepted the sacrifice of Abel, but He did not accept the sacrifice of Cain. Rather than seeing his problem as a problem with God, Cain surmised his problem was with his brother. The end result of his thought processes was murder. Because of his inability to handle what he perceived as God's rejection, he focused his anger at God towards his brother. Again, the transgression brought a greater separation from God. Cain became a wanderer without a place or land, which is the sign of a curse. He had no sense of belonging or attachment. He was marked *by* God, but not marked *for* God. This seems so descriptive of much of the church today. God is now calling us to our place and purpose. We need to prepare ourselves and respond to the call of God in these days. It is God's heart of mercy that longs to bring the "wanderer" home.

LOSING SIGHT OF YOUR PURPOSE

The ministry of the Son of God is a ministry congested with struggle at every corner. His struggle and ours is against the power of darkness that has resulted from the fall of man. It is a struggle to obey the Father's will so that the Kingdom of God will be established in our lives and in the earth, and it is a struggle we must not bear alone. We were meant to share that burden with others. The purpose of God in the earth is not a "one-man show." If it was, Jesus Christ Himself could have done the whole job when He was here. This purpose can only be fulfilled in the Church, which is His Body. All of us are to be unique and vital members of the Body, but no *one* member is to be the head. This position belongs only to the Lord Himself. How can we struggle *with* one another, when we are so often in a struggle *against* one another? This is the day when God is calling us to a higher purpose.

It is easy in any conflict to forget the goal and purpose of our struggle. The pressure of a particular battle can cause us to lose sight of the overall objectives. This is what happened to Adam and Eve. In their struggle to fulfill their purpose, they were convinced God was the cause of their conflict rather than the source of their strength. They lost sight of their purpose. This is also what happened to Cain when in his struggle, he turned on his brother rather than dealing with God.

As a pastor, I have often witnessed people going through struggle and conflict, who forget what the purpose of their struggle was for or what it was against. These people are at odds with the very God they had set out to serve, or they are at odds with the people God has called them to serve with. Many defeated people in the Body of Christ have fallen because they've lost focus of their purpose and destiny. Many of these people sit on the sidelines of life, victims of their own loss of vision and purpose.

Life is a struggle. One needs to only look at the natural world and see the endless strife in the world. For the most part, this discord is the result of the fall of man. This struggle can end only when God redeems the earth from its impending destruction through His anointed sons who will take their place of dominion in the earth. We must take our place! We must go forth with a focused purpose and destiny. The greatest obstacle to overcome in this area of our struggle is *with* people. The fulfillment of the law of God can only come when we see it has a twofold aspect. It involves our relationship with God and also our relationships with one another. We must understand that there are no private journeys. We are all vitally linked to one another.

Love—A Mighty Weapon in the Hands of God's People

He said to him, "What is written in the law? What is your reading of it?" So he answered and said, " 'You shall love the

72

Lord your God with all your heart, with all your soul, with all your strength, and with all your mind,' and 'your neighbor as yourself'" (Luke 10:26-27).

We can only imagine the great power of God that will be loosed when we operate in this sphere of love for God and one another. In the "love chapter," First Corinthians 13, we get a glimpse of what will happen. This chapter tells us that the gifts of God operate, in part, because they are motivated by love. Love gives power and energy to our actions in this world.

Love never fails. But whether there are prophecies, they will fail; whether there are tongues, they will cease; whether there is knowledge, it will vanish away. For we know in part and we prophesy in part (1 Corinthians 13:8-9).

It goes on to say that when love becomes perfected, the partial operation will give way to the fullness. God has given us certain gifts to accomplish His plans, and those gifts can only grow into perfection by the power of love.

But when that which is perfect has come, then that which is in part will be done away (1 Corinthians 13:10).

The gifts that once were used as play toys to amuse us now become the reality they were meant to be in the beginning. This fullness is linked with our own personal development in the process of becoming the person God has called us to be.

*When I was a child, I spoke as a child, I understood as a child, I thought as a child; but when I became a man, I put away childish things. For now we see in a mirror, dimly, but then face to face. **Now I know in part, but then I shall know just as I also am known*** (1 Corinthians 13:11-12, emphasis added).

Once we have the proper love for God and one another, we can move forward as the sons of God. Just as it was with Jesus, the firstborn Son, it will likewise be a journey that will lead us into the world of man to demonstrate the love of God for those who live a life of pain and rejection. Jesus was sent into the world from the Father's love, and He lived by the motivation of this love. If Jesus would have gone forth, not knowing where He came from and where He was going, He could have easily become an enemy to those He came to help. The struggle of His ministry could have caused Him to lose sight of His purpose and motivation. Rather than dying for a cause, He could have been tempted to kill for His cause. Rather than minister to sinners, He could have become enraged by their condition and fought against them. Instead of becoming an enemy of the sinner, though, Jesus was the enemy of sin. He clearly saw His purpose, for it was not clouded by personal needs and aspirations.

TAPPING INTO FATHER'S LOVE

I understand that it is not easy to walk in this kind of love. In fact, if you don't have it, you cannot express it. Divine love does not naturally generate from us; it must be given to us by the Father. I have found in the ministry that it can be very easy to lose focus of the real enemy. When helping a person caught in sin, we need to stay focused on the real problem. If the person doesn't change quickly, it becomes easy to see them as the enemy, and we can become agitated with them. This is a good time to step back and see if you are living by the power of your own natural resources or if you have tapped into Father's love. Remember that His love is patient and kind.

If a person is walking in self-destructive behavior, anyone desiring to help them can become their enemy. This is what Paul wanted young Timothy to understand as he set out to minister.

And a servant of the Lord must not quarrel but be gentle to all, able to teach, patient, in humility correcting those who are in opposition, if God perhaps will grant them repentance, so that they may know the truth (2 Timothy 2:24-25).

We must approach our relationships with others as a servant of the Lord. We can't take this struggle personally. We can't fight with the people who are already fighting with themselves—they don't need another enemy. They need instruction and patience and gentle care. Time is the greatest contributor to the success of God's purpose. Have you ever noticed how many in the church are always predicting God's judgment, and yet He doesn't seem to follow through with our puny predictions? God is patient. Time is not His enemy; it is ours.

Humility becomes our greatest asset as we serve others and seek to bring them the Father's love. When we remember that we came from God and that our righteousness is a gift of God, we will not need to judge the motivation of another person, nor will we find fault with them. We know that we did not do a thing to earn our good standing with God, so why should we seek to lay heavy burdens on others? We must patiently direct them to the same mercy and grace of God that rescued us.

Humility will produce meekness. We must help people where they are, not standing over them, but standing with them. The struggle to help others should not create within us a struggle to prove our methods or ourselves. The person in need should remain our focus.

SPIRITUAL SONS KNOW
HOW TO EFFECTIVELY CORRECT THE OPPOSITION

With our identity in God fully settled and with Father's love entrenched in our hearts, we can be pure instruments to "correct" those in opposition to the Father's purposes. To help people, we must sometimes stand in opposition to them. Once our motives and purpose are established, we can operate like Jesus did. He often had to stand in opposition to those He loved in order to help them fulfill the purpose of the Father. Jesus had a great relationship with His disciples. He loved them; but even though He loved them, He was not reluctant to stand in opposition to them when it was necessary. In Matthew 16, while conversing with His disciples, Jesus asked them a very important question: "Who are people saying I am?" They replied that some thought He was Elias or Jeremiah, the prophet. Then came the most important question of all: "Who do you think I am?" Peter responded, "You are the Christ, the Son of the living God." Jesus then told him, "You know this only because the Father has revealed it to you."

Peter must have felt very empowered by this revelation knowledge. Right after this powerful response, Jesus then went on to describe how He would need to die for the sins of the world. Peter jumped in, as the great defender of truth and quite proud of his spiritual wisdom, and declared that Jesus would not die. Peter was going to protect Him. Although Peter's proclamation was noble, it was contrary to the will of God. It was also most likely motivated by his own pride. Jesus responded by rebuking him.

> But He turned and said to Peter, "Get behind Me, Satan! You are an offense to Me, for you are not mindful of the things of God, but the things of men." Then Jesus said to His disciples, "If anyone desires to come after Me, let him deny himself, and take up his cross, and follow Me" (Matthew 16:23-24).

There will be times in the journey when a course correction will be necessary. There will be times when we are giving that correction, and there will probably be times when we are receiving it. We don't need a church of patronizing friends if we are to do the thing God wants us to do. Church should be a place of mutual care even when it means the painful extraction of things that are hindering our journey. For too long, the church has been a place of superficial relationships rather than speaking the truth in love. We need true friends who will help us in the pursuit of the Kingdom of God. True friends will recognize that the road which leads to spiritual authority will require support and encouragement, but they will also be willing to tell us what we don't want to hear. A true friend will help the Father work in our lives to bring us to perfection or completion in God.

> As iron sharpens iron, so a man sharpens the countenance of his friend (Proverbs 27:17).

Just as Jesus refused to be patronized, so He certainly did not patronize Peter. Peter was not seeing clearly, and he needed to know it. Sadly, he was more on the side of the enemy than on the side of His Master. Many church conflicts could be avoided if friends would be friends and keep needless flesh works in check. We should be confronting the powers of this world, but instead we are in constant conflict with one another.

Also detrimental to growing up in Christ is to strengthen friendship bonds by seditious actions of joining with one another against other people. Taking sides in conflict is not the way to strengthen bonds of friendship. Taking sides is the way to give the devil dominion in our lives and in the church. In His own situation, Jesus was determined to end this conflict then and there. "Peter, don't tell Me what I want to hear; tell Me what I need to hear." He certainly let Peter know the truth. Of course, we need to be sensitive to one another and show our love, but sensitivity and love need to be tempered with the truth.

> *But, speaking the truth in love, may grow up in all things into Him who is the head—Christ....And be kind to one another, tenderhearted, forgiving one another, even as God in Christ forgave you* (Ephesians 4:15,32).

God never intended for us to face the struggle of life alone. This is why He declared in the beginning:

> *And the Lord God said, "It is not good that man should be alone; I will make him a helper comparable to him"* (Genesis 2:18).

GOD GAVE YOU MANY HELPERS

The word *helper*, in the original Greek text, means someone to give us aid by surrounding and guarding something. However, it is not a good choice of words for this verse. The word in this Scripture actually means someone to stand opposite of, or the opposite part. With regard to man, it was a woman created by God. In many ways, women are the opposite of men. They often present an opposing view so that together, they—man and woman—can find the truth.

One author popularized that men are from Mars and women are from Venus. Well, in truth, we are from the same planet; yet, we have certainly been created differently. Men and women tend to see life differently. One is not right and the other wrong—just different. Together, by blending the different perspectives, we will be able to fulfill our original purpose. In all our relationships, we should be of the understanding that in order to be complete, we need help from people who are our opposites. We don't need "yes" people in our lives; we need people who will guard and surround us even when that means standing in opposition to us. All relationships will encounter conflict—it is the nature of living together in this world. But this conflict can produce the purpose of God in our lives. In the friction, we are refined and prepared for our destiny.

Because we need people different than ourselves, and also because God has uniquely formed each and every one of us for His purpose, we need to effectively deal with the conflicts that our differences cause. Most Christians choose the easy way out by demanding that every person be the same, or by simply walking away from the conflict. We tend to fellowship with only those like ourselves and exclude those who are different. Unfortunately, we not only exclude them from our fellowship, we also try to exclude one another from the Kingdom. It is time to go on to maturity, and that means be willing to confront our differences in the spirit of the Father's love. This will bring Father's favor in our midst.

As mature people, we will seek to resolve our conflicts with the purpose of finding the truth rather than winning the argument. The Scriptures teach us that our ability to make friends even with our enemies is the truest indicator of our spiritual maturity. Paul addressed this issue with the church in Corinth. He told them in the opening of the Book of First Corinthians, that they have all the gifts in operation, the best of the teachers, and also the best teaching. But in spite of all the ways the Corinthian church excelled, Paul still considered them spiritually immature. Why?

> *And I, brethren, could not speak to you as to spiritual people but as to carnal, as to babes in Christ. I fed you with milk and not with solid food; for until now you were not able to receive it, and even now you are still not able; for you are still carnal. For where there are envy, strife, and divisions among you, are you not carnal and behaving like mere men?* (1 Corinthians 3:1-3)

The sign of their immaturity was their inability to deal with the conflicts in relationships. Conflict is not a problem with God.

But an unwillingness to face those conflicts will hinder us from reaching our full potential and will certainly restrict us from being the sons of God in the earth. Growing up as sons means that we will embrace the conflicts that come into our life, and together we will come into the perfect place of the Father's plans.

Chapter Six

I Came to Bring a Sword—
Facing Life's Conflicts

Do not think that I came to bring peace on earth. I did not come to bring peace but a sword....He who finds his life will lose it, and he who loses his life for My sake will find it (Matthew 10:34,39).

Once we have dealt with the issue of personal confrontation in the Body, we are ready to face the confrontation with the world system. The process of conflict strengthens us in order that we will be qualified to assist in the establishment of our Father's Kingdom. If we don't learn how to handle personal confrontation that comes against us early in our Christian journey, then we will not be able to handle the larger tests that will come later. This is why so many people head out to do great things for God but then become personally bankrupt in the process. Even the apostle Paul was mindful of his need for constant personal self-evaluation as he sought to always maintain the integrity of his ministry.

Therefore I run thus: not with uncertainty. Thus I fight: not as one who beats the air. But I discipline my body and bring it into subjection, lest, when I have preached to others, I myself should become disqualified (1 Corinthians 9:26-27).

Jesus was always fully prepared for any public confrontation that might come His way because He had faced His own private and personal issues earlier in life. He had resolved the issue of personal identity and had overcome the subtle issues of satanic confrontations. We must always be vigilant so we do not give place to the devil. Never think that once you have won a battle, you are at the end of the war.

"Be angry, and do not sin": do not let the sun go down on your wrath, nor give place to the devil (Ephesians 4:26-27).

IN THIS LIFE YOU WILL HAVE TROUBLE

Paul declared that while true spiritual sons will at times experience negative reactions to life's situations, they will not let the problems linger. They will confront them immediately so that they do not fester and eventually poison them.

Why do many Christians think that when someone encounters a problem on the way to their destiny, they must have missed God? We've already noted that the Spirit led Jesus into the wilderness immediately after His baptism and recognition by His Father. He was led by the Spirit right into the lion's den to confront the enemy. Many times in the church when problems arise, there is a question as to whether someone heard from God, or worse, that surely the judgment of God is upon that person. This simplistic evaluation and judgmental responses are indicators of spiritual immaturity. Jesus made it very clear when He declared that in this life all will have tribulation. The issue is not, "Will we have conflict and trouble in this life?" but "How will we deal with the trouble that confronts us?"

We have a Father in Heaven looking to enlist sons who are willing to confront the obstacles that stand in the way of advancing the Kingdom and who will pull down strongholds that prevent that expansion. Unfortunately, as soon as the process begins, many people begin to doubt God or the servant of God who is trying to push forward against the opposing ones. When the Lord created His first sons, He told them to be fruitful, multiply, fill up the earth, and "take dominion." Obviously, the earth had some obstacles for the sons of God to overcome! In order to "take dominion," we will have to persevere against those who have seized portions of Father's world and who are seeking to resist us.

CONQUERING YOUR INNER TERRITORY

Once we have taken control of our inner territory, then we are firmly established so that we can go forth to take the Kingdom. When Jesus came into the world, He came to break the power of satan and develop a generation of sons who would be willing to take the spoils of the plundered house of satan.

> *Or how can one enter a strong man's house and plunder his goods, unless he first binds the strong man? And then he will plunder his house. He who is not with Me is against Me, and he who does not gather with Me scatters abroad* (Matthew 12:29-30).

It is not that we are immobilized to move forward until we are perfect on the inside, but it has certainly been our lack of personal control that has limited our authority in God. If we are not in control of our inner territory, how can we become successful with the outward battles around us? If we are having trouble dealing with our issues in the Body of Christ, how will we survive with the world?

> *If you have run with the footmen and they have wearied you, then how can you contend with horses? And if in the land of peace, in which you trusted, they wearied you, then how will you do in the floodplain of the Jordan?* (Jeremiah 12:5)

It is time for us to buckle up, make our advance against the systems of this world, and become the men and women who will rescue those who are drowning in a world of hurt and pain. But we will never become those men and women until we have allowed the Father to heal our own inner sorrow and hurts.

WHISTLE WHILE YOU WORK

In the beginning, mankind was given a mandate from God to take dominion of the earth. Adam and his wife, Eve, were given a specific mandate when God placed them in the Garden of Eden— the responsibility for the care of the garden; they were to guard and cultivate it. After the great fall, resulting from their disobedience, the land was cursed with thorns and thistles. In spite of the curse, they were never relieved of their responsibility. However, God promises to bring His people into a rest that will empower them in a new way to fulfill this divinely inspired responsibility. Man begins his work in the place of rest so that he can whistle while he works.

In other words, God takes the sting out of the labor, but He doesn't take away the work or responsibility that was originally given to him. We are called as colaborers to work together with God and one another.

The work that is given to us will always involve problems. The issue is, how will we handle those problems? But in our skepticism, we might ask ourselves the question, "How could the garden be a delightful land if there was work to do?" Unfortunately, our stunted perspectives hinder us from finding and fulfilling the purposes of God for our lives.

TAKING STEWARDSHIP OF YOUR OWN GARDEN

The problem is that as baby Christians, we always want God to create what we consider to be the perfect conditions for our lives. We think that the ultimate situation for us is a life where we are *comfortable* in the work of God. We want to create a world that is to our making rather than accepting the world that God has created for us.

God created mankind with a desire for dominion and with a desire to find and fulfill his purpose in life. Until we understand this truth, we will continue to struggle and never know what will bring us true contentment in life. Both men and women at all levels of society are motivated by a desire to exercise dominion over something. This is why God gives to each and every one of us an area of dominion. Our spheres of influence may be different, but inherent in our nature is the desire to steward what has been given to us. Our faithfulness to our little place of dominion will determine if that "garden" will grow into a larger sphere of influence. On the other hand, an unfaithful steward will not be given a larger sphere of influence in the garden of God, and they may even risk losing their stewardship!

One day, I read an article that said the average man lives less than five years after retirement. As I contemplated this reality, several thoughts came to me. We naturally think that the secret to longevity is rest from work when in fact it is finding work with a purpose. Your life was created to have a purpose other than your personal satisfaction and comfort. Without purpose, it is clear that our physical condition deteriorates. The body was built for meaningful use. If you don't exercise, you will lose your health. This is the message the medical community has been trying to get across to American society, but it certainly is one we don't want to hear. However, if we refuse to hear, it will be to our detriment. The same is true of our spiritual self. If we want to be strong, we must exercise; and it must be exercise that is focused in the right direction.

LEARNING TO HEAR GOD'S VOICE

For everyone who partakes only of milk is unskilled in the word of righteousness, for he is a babe. But solid food belongs to those who are of full age, that is, those who by reason of use have their senses exercised to discern both good and evil (Hebrews 5:13-14).

When I was young in the Lord, I was intrigued by the fact that man could hear God, and when I received the baptism of the Holy Spirit at the age of 17, my next goal was to hear the voice of God for myself. I remember the first time God spoke to me. I was in a service where they were taking up a special offering for the building fund. The Lord spoke and told me to give $100. It was 1972 and I was still in high school...and $100 was a whole lot of money. I said to myself, *This must be the flesh*; I thought that it could have been the devil trying to test me. In those days, in my eagerness to know God, I had already visited many churches; and although one church in particular had exciting miracle services, it seemed that there was always some scam taking place there to get money from people. I remember one day in particular when the preacher said that God told him to tell everyone to give their biggest bill and their smallest piece of change as an offering. I had a twenty-dollar bill in my wallet. And I needed that to take out the girl I was with! I learned that day that when you go to church, you leave your wallet at home.

85

Well, these thoughts were on my mind as I considered the tug to give the $100. I paid my tithes faithfully but was very suspicious of somebody trying to get extra money out of me. But if this was God asking me for the $100, how could I refuse? I needed to respond for I truly knew this to be the voice of God.

As is so often the case in my life, obedience opened the door to a new dimension in God. I began to hear from God in a brand-new way as He was now beginning to establish me in the ministry of a prophet. But I do remember that my thinking in those days was really out of whack. I believed the better I heard the voice of God, the less problems I would have in life. It made sense to me at the time. But there were many promises in the Scriptures that I could point to regarding divine blessing for those who are obedient, and I had learned the power and blessing of obedience in my life. I could personally testify how walking in obedience brings divine blessing. For me obedience was the safest and easiest way to walk. The Word declares:

> *Good understanding gains favor, but the way of the unfaithful is hard* (Proverbs 13:15).

Over the years when I heard people complain about how hard it was to be a Christian, I was offended by their lack of honor towards God. Indeed, my obedience had filled my life with blessing. Yet, there is a place in God where we move not on our own behalf, but on God's—a place where we will encounter opposition. When applied to our personal life, the walk in the Word is one of blessing and prosperity. Yet, when the Father wants to teach us, as the sons of God, or wants us to take one of His burdens, a different mind-set must be involved. This is the suffering we do for Christ. It is this suffering that will lead us into the glory of God.

SUFFERING THAT BRINGS GLORY

And if children, then heirs—heirs of God and joint heirs with Christ, if indeed we suffer with Him, that we may also be glorified together. For I consider that the sufferings of this present time are not worthy to be compared with the glory which shall be revealed in us (Romans 8:17-18).

For to you it has been granted on behalf of Christ, not only to believe in Him, but also to suffer for His sake (Philippians 1:29).

You will show me the path of life; in Your presence is fullness of joy; at Your right hand are pleasures forevermore (Psalm 16:11).

Suffering should not be glorified nor sought after; but as we press the claims of our King against the forces of this world, there will be resistance. Paul, the great apostle, had suffered dearly for the sake of the gospel, but in his suffering, he had learned a great truth. Glory grows in the soil of suffering. The suffering of those who are breaking down the doors of satan's strongholds creates a pathway of glorious restoration. Tertullian, one of the early church fathers, said that the blood of the martyrs is the seed of the Church.

Down through the ages, men and women, the true sons of God, have been called upon to suffer harshly for the sake of the Kingdom and for the honor of their King. They have found great grace in their trials, and they have unleashed glory through their suffering.

Take My yoke upon you and learn from Me, for I am gentle and lowly in heart, and you will find rest for your souls. For My yoke is easy and My burden is light (Matthew 11:29-30).

Once we recognize that suffering is not our goal in God but simply a part of the process, then we are ready for service as the sons of God. We must understand that every true son will face opposition. Sometimes that opposition will be intense. Sometimes it might even come from those of our own household. But no matter what comes at us, we must be seeking the power of the Kingdom of God.

I do want to point out that not all suffering is for the sake of the Kingdom. Sometimes we create our own suffering by going our own way. This will not bring glory to Father, only shame.

LEADERSHIP IS CONFRONTATION

When I first began to pastor, I had already heard a lot of people complain over the years about churches and pastors, and I figured I would do it right. All the unhappy people would now have a pastor who loved them and a church that cared for them. What a happy flock of sheep we were going to be...or so I thought. It certainly sounds naive to many; but how could I fail with an honest heart and the ability to hear from God?

I remember talking to pastor James Beall of the Bethesda Christian Church about my concerns. He said, "Loren, leadership is confrontation." That was a revelation for me! I didn't even like confrontation. I thought leadership was standing before the people, not standing against them. You would have thought I hadn't ever read the Bible. Paul wrote this same admonition to a fainthearted leader named Timothy.

> *And a servant of the Lord must not quarrel but be gentle to all, able to teach, patient, in humility correcting those who are in opposition, if God perhaps will grant them repentance, so that they may know the truth* (2 Timothy 2:24-25).

Once we understand that confrontation is inevitable for a leader, the first area of confrontation then becomes the people we are called to help. If you're going to help people, you must sometimes stand in opposition to them. I found out early on, if you want to help someone who is an enemy to themselves, you will appear to them as the enemy. You are not really their personal enemy, but simply the enemy of their affliction or the thing that has them bound. We are living in a day when both the world and the Church have need of strong leadership. We need leaders who will tell us what we need to hear, not what we want to hear. When we want teachers who tell us what we want to hear rather than what we need to hear, we are like those who have itchy ears.

> *For the time will come when they will not endure sound doctrine, but according to their own desires, because they have itching ears, they will heap up for themselves teachers; and they will turn their ears away from the truth, and be turned aside to fables* (2 Timothy 4:3-4).

We don't need leaders with itchy ears ministering to people with the same problem. We need leaders who will bring forth that which is necessary for the edification and maturity of the Church. It is only the truth of God that will release the power of God in our lives. If we are not careful, we will be those who exchange the truth of God for a lie. This will result in the judgment of God and cause us to lose God's blessing.

> *Therefore God also gave them up to uncleanness, in the lusts of their hearts, to dishonor their bodies among themselves, who exchanged the truth of God for the lie, and worshiped and served the creature rather than the Creator, who is blessed forever. Amen* (Romans 1:24-25).

FINDING A GOOD HELPER FOR THE JOURNEY

When God created Adam, the first man, he needed a helper. God created him a "help meet." As we have said in the last chapter, the word "helper," in the original Greek text, means to guard, surround, and protect. This does not imply a passive helper. Eve would have to be strong if she were to fulfill this role. The word "meet" is from a word that means to stand boldly opposite of, or against someone. Sometimes to protect someone, we must protect them from themselves. You must stand in opposition. Many a woman has helped to deliver her husband from a road of destruction through fulfilling this role. The religious community has always sought to destroy the strength of women, when in fact, we need to empower them for the purposes God has for them. We don't need weaker women to save our marriages, but we do need stronger men. Through cultural misconceptions of the Word, we have enslaved women. Remember, God is not looking for slaves; He is looking for sons. It is our differences that often cause conflict, but in this conflict we are all transformed into a more perfect and unified image.

If you read your Bible without cultural bias, you will see God always releasing women, not enslaving them. Sarah is mentioned in the Bible as the example of submission to her husband, Abraham. She is indeed a godly example. Yet, when you read the story of Abraham and Sarah, it is very clear she was not a wimp. She spoke when necessary and certainly had influence on Abraham's walk with God. It should be noted as well that God would not allow the

Word to come to pass in Abraham's life without Sarah being a part of the plan.

Just as Abraham did, many of us are always looking for the "right" person to accomplish something in our lives that will make it easier on us, rather than desiring the thing that will bring out the best in us. When we have a change of attitude and mind-set, there will be a lot less church hopping and divorces and a lot more spiritual authority from God exercised over our lives. We will be joining ourselves to those who will truly be our help, rather than the ones who simply make us feel comfortable.

LET US SIT DOWN AND REASON TOGETHER

Keep in mind, when I speak of conflict, I am not speaking of arguments and debate. Once we establish that our life is not just about attaining our personal satisfaction but fulfilling our divine purpose, we can approach an issue without emotional agendas. When you want to know truth, you understand you need a broad perspective. You understand that you are not the fountain of all truth and that others will add to your life what you lack. You set yourself to listen. You don't own your ideas, and you don't have an ax to grind. You are not afraid someone is going to take your place or usurp your authority. Like Jesus, the Son of God, you will accept the initiative to communicate by getting into the other person's world and with a heart of compassion be sensitive to their thoughts and feelings.

Does it sound impossible? Jesus set the example; and when we become mature, we will certainly be able to operate in this realm. It is only when we learn to settle our personal confrontations with one another that we are ready to go forth and confront the greater responsibilities God has for us.

Often, whenever we think of a person who is spiritual, we think of a person who prophesies, quotes a lot of Bible verses, or spends a lot of time in prayer. In our minds the spiritual person is far removed from the mundane experiences of life. Yet, when we see the life of Jesus, the most spiritual person who ever lived, a man of prayer and spiritual gifts, we find the significant thing about His life was His relationship with people. Watch how He interacted with those around Him. Watch how He treated the sick and wounded. Observe how He related to the religious leaders. Notice how He took time with His disciples.

Many great prophets had come and worked miracles for the people. And many messengers had come from God to speak to the people. But what set Jesus apart, of course, was that He was not just a messenger of God; He was God revealed in the flesh. Yet, in demonstration He came not just to show us *the works* of the Father, but He came to show us the Father. *He didn't come to show us how to be God; He came to show us how God could be a man.* In showing us this side of God, He gave to us a beautiful picture of how we can live and demonstrate God to our world. This was His purpose and His message. It is this purpose that demonstrates the level of our spiritual maturity.

Paul tried to make the Corinthian church understand this. He wrote to them as a church that had all the spiritual gifts, the best of preachers, and a profound understanding of the Word. Yet, when he wrote to them, he said he had to write to them as babes in Christ. They were carnal and not spiritual. Why did he see them in this light? He saw them this way because of their relationships with one another.

> *I fed you with milk and not with solid food; for until now you were not able to receive it, and even now you are still not able; for you are still carnal. For where there are envy, strife, and divisions among you, are you not carnal and behaving like mere men? For when one says, "I am of Paul," and another, "I am of Apollos," are you not carnal?* (1 Corinthians 3:2-4)

Everyone wanted to be right and associated with the "best" teacher. They were insecure so they were seeking their notoriety in whom they knew or were associated with. Does this sound familiar?

EVEN WITH OUR ISSUES, GLORIFY GOD

We need to confront the issues of conflict in our relationships with one another. It is sad to think how often Christians ignore this responsibility. Jesus instructed us to take the initiative in this area, even when it involves someone with whom we don't have an issue but who may have a problem with us.

Therefore if you bring your gift to the altar, and there remember that your brother has something against you, leave your gift there before the altar, and go your way. First be reconciled to your brother, and then come and offer your gift. Agree with your adversary quickly, while you are on the way with him, lest your adversary deliver you to the judge, the judge hand you over to the officer, and you be thrown into prison (Matthew 5:23-25).

Often rather than confront situations or problems with one another, we choose to ignore them. The end result is that a root begins to grow within that eventually brings death—a root of bitterness. Ignoring problems never makes them go away; they only get bigger.

Pursue peace with all people, and holiness, without which no one will see the Lord: looking carefully lest anyone fall short of the grace of God; lest any root of bitterness springing up cause trouble, and by this many become defiled (Hebrews 12:14-15).

Sowing Death or Sowing Life

If we do not confront the people we have issues with, we have no right to expect anything from them. The full weight of the problem falls upon us. Sometimes people use the excuse of bad experiences in the past or even their upbringing to justify not dealing with issues. In any case, the judgment still comes to you. An even more severe judgment comes when you fail to confront the problem and instead go and share your bitterness with others rather than directly with the person you have the conflict with. This simply makes you a sower of discord and will certainly bring judgment upon you.

These six things the Lord hates, yes, seven are an abomination to Him....a false witness who speaks lies, and one who sows discord among brethren (Proverbs 6:16,19).

You may feel totally justified in your feelings, but if you're sharing them with someone other than the person you have the problem with, you are sowing death. If you are hurting, you need to deal with the problem—not run around looking for sympathy. This artificial medicating of your pain will only cause it to be aggravated.

ARE YOU CONFRONTING YOUR PROBLEMS OR RUNNING FROM THEM?

The increase in the rate of divorce at the present time is alarming. This is a mirror of the condition of our society—a society looking for greater fulfillment out of life. We are more concerned about what a relationship brings to us rather than what we can bring to a relationship. We are more concerned about how others can serve us rather than how we can serve others. And when we bring these ingredients into a marriage, it is a recipe for disaster.

I believe God wants us to confront the issues of our relationships so we can have good marriages. God is not just against divorce; He is also opposed to bad marriages! This does not mean that people can think they are confronting the problem by getting out of their marriages. That is not confrontation; that's running. We have a responsibility to deal with problems before they get so overwhelming we want to run from them. It is time for the Church to come to this higher level of confrontation and judgment so we can have the blessings God wants us to have in life. However, this blessing will only come with responsibility. Are you a son or a child? Are you going to sit and complain, or are you going to stand and be counted? Jesus had no problem with confronting issues. Motivated by a heart of love, He rose up to face the most difficult issues in His day. Look how He dealt with the unbelief in His own disciples; watch how He lovingly confronted them in order to lift them up into a higher realm of spiritual reality.

Dealing with relationship issues can be a cumbersome experience. We often structure our lives to avoid any possible conflict. We would rather have rules and regulations that protect us from conflict. Don't give us a relationship; we are afraid of that. We only want to relate from a structural level rather than a relational one. Paul didn't claim authority over the Corinthian church as an apostle; he claimed his authority because he was their father. It is only when we begin to relate on this level that the Church will reach its highest potential and only then will we truly find the satisfying life.

All over the world, ministers are hungering for relationships, and all they are offered is another organization. Even when we start to build gatherings based on relationship, it isn't long before someone is organizing them into a structure that eliminates relational interaction. When are we going to see the light and quit working against ourselves? When we truly realize God's way is the best way.

God begins His action in our lives from a relationship perspective, and He will end with a relationship perspective! God's way of reaching His divine plans is through people. But whenever people are involved, there will be conflict. That conflict does not have to be bad, however; it can become a process that increases our spiritual maturity and brings us the Father's favor.

Chapter Seven

Getting to the Heart of the Matter

And Jesus said to him, "Today salvation has come to this house, because he also is a son of Abraham; for the Son of Man has come to seek and to save that which was lost" (Luke 19:9-10).

Confrontation is a necessary component of the ministry of the sons of God. Because we live in a world that is in rebellion against God's purposes and because sin has trapped the residents of this planet in bondage, the sons of God will always be in conflict with those opposing forces. Not only must we confront the problems within our own lives and the problems of the people we have come to serve, but we must also confront the opposition against the work God, the Father, has given us to do.

Isn't it amazing that the greatest opposition Jesus faced was not from the secular world but from the religious establishment? The apostle Paul made it clear that the sons of God are the ones who are led by the Spirit of God. Interestingly, the idea of being led by the Spirit is not one the religious establishment feels comfortable with. They would much rather be in control of every person and every situation for fear of losing their place and their power. Even the idea of revival is a threat to an established religious system.

Because of the freshness of spiritual encounters that comes with revival, people are more open to reexamine the spiritual reality of the religious system. This sometimes leads to the reexamining of the institution they are a part of. How ironic it has been that throughout church history, every time God has wanted to move in a fresh or new way, He has had to raise up a new group of people to hear His voice; and most often these people are outside the religious walls. The problem with the voice of God is that it threatens our way of doing things. It asks us to abandon things that we don't want to give up. It requires us to look at our motives and get out of our comfort zones. This kind of spiritual climate challenges us to evaluate our religious securities, theological opinions, and spiritual realities. This is what the new order of God always does. He comes to confront us so that He might change and raise up a new generation of "Joshuas" and "Calebs" who are prepared to stand against the prevailing opinions and move forward in the purposes of God.

CONFRONTING THE RELIGIOUS SYSTEM

As Jesus ministered to the people, the crowds were amazed at the manner in which He spoke. There was a resonating authority in His speech indicating a deeper spiritual reality than they had ever encountered. Unlike the scribes and the Pharisees, Jesus not only spoke the Word, He was the Word. He embodied the very message that He delivered with such power, and that Word was confirmed with miraculous works that amazed the people. The people were moved deeply by their encounter with this Man, and this popular shift towards Jesus was a threat to the leaders. So what did they do? They did everything they could to find fault with Jesus and His doctrine. If they couldn't stop Him on religious grounds, they were willing to bring the Roman authorities against Him on political grounds.

It is an ironic twist, but in order to heal the hurting masses around us, we often have to fight the religious establishment to do so. The ones who claim to be seeking the will of God are often at odds with that very will. This was true in the time of Christ and has proven true throughout church history.

I have found it to be true in my own life. When I was young, I grew up in a typical, small, American church. We often claimed to have a desire for evangelism, and we would have our share of special events and new programs for reaching the lost. Everything would fall into place, we thought, and we would eventually win our community. But we never found a program or event that produced results. The problem, we would reason, must be the program, or worse than that, maybe God just wasn't moving in that way any longer. Looking at church history, we could easily conclude there are times of revival and times when there isn't revival. It was just not the time. It was easy to come to these kinds of conclusions to excuse our lack of success.

WHERE IS YOUR HEART?

What we failed to perceive, however, were the true sources of the problem. We failed to look at our heart motivations and our spiritual bondage to the old system. You can say you want God to move, but if your heart isn't right, you will end up fighting against the very plans you yourself have set in motion. This was the way of the children of Israel in the time of the ministry of Isaiah, the prophet.

> *The whole vision has become to you like the words of a book that is sealed, which men deliver to one who is literate, saying, "Read this, please." And he says, "I cannot, for it is sealed." Then the book is delivered to one who is illiterate, saying, "Read this, please." And he says, "I am not literate." Therefore the Lord said: "Inasmuch as these people draw near with their mouths and honor Me with their lips, but have removed their hearts far from Me, and their fear toward Me is taught by the commandment of men (Isaiah 29:11-13).*

The great prophet Isaiah defines, in these verses, the very essence of a false religious system. It has the right word, doctrine, and plan...but no heart. Its plans and programs are shared and communicated with zeal, yet because the heart is not a part of the program, all the seemingly right things end up becoming a snare to those who share it. They appear right and righteous to the leaders, but to God they are dead men's bones. While trapped within the system, we cannot see the true nature of our hearts nor understand how far away we have drifted from the passion and compassion of our life with God.

BLIND EYES AND WHITEWASHED TOMBS

Woe to you, scribes and Pharisees, hypocrites! For you cleanse the outside of the cup and dish, but inside they are full of extortion and self-indulgence. Blind Pharisee, first cleanse the inside of the cup and dish, that the outside of them may be clean also. Woe to you, scribes and Pharisees, hypocrites! For you are like whitewashed tombs which indeed appear beautiful outwardly, but inside are full of dead men's bones and all uncleanness (Matthew 23:25-27).

We spend so much time trying to develop a system based upon programs and constant activity that we forget true Christianity is of the heart, not the letter. I am sure the Pharisees thought themselves to be righteous before God. They never saw their motives as evil or misguided. They resisted the ministry of Jesus Christ and eventually sought His crucifixion, thinking that they were doing the right thing. Yet, they never fully realized the tragic impact of what they were doing.

Seeking to protect the system, they ended up fighting against God. It is easy to look at the stories of the Bible and think that these religious leaders as well as the people were intentionally resisting God. Yet, this was not the case. The truth is, they were committed to rigorously keeping all of the law and fulfilling all the demands of Scriptures. They carefully examined every action that they took, and they equally scrutinized the actions of others. The problem was that they put all their attention upon the outward observances of the law without understanding what was in their heart. They had the appearance of being righteous because they were doing the right thing, but in their hearts was much envy and evil.

While intending to do something for God, they actually became the enemies of God. This should scare us into humility! We should be crying out for God's mercy and grace at all times, lest we fall to the same end. It is possible that we are not fully aware of what is in our hearts.

Why couldn't they see the error of their way? They could not see because God had hidden it from them. If we claim to be one thing and practice another, God declares He will blind us so we can't see, and plug our ears so we can't hear the truth.

> *Pause and wonder! Blind yourselves and be blind! They are drunk, but not with wine; they stagger, but not with intoxicating drink. For the Lord has poured out on you the spirit of deep sleep, and has closed your eyes, namely, the prophets; and He has covered your heads, namely, the seers* (Isaiah 29:9-10).

This was indeed the condition of the Pharisees in the time of Christ.

> *And in them the prophecy of Isaiah is fulfilled, which says: "Hearing you will hear and shall not understand, and seeing you will see and not perceive; for the hearts of this people have grown dull. Their ears are hard of hearing, and their eyes they have closed, lest they should see with their eyes and hear with their ears, lest they should understand with their hearts and turn, so that I should heal them"* (Matthew 13:14-15).

Spiritual blindness is the natural condition of those who resist the move of God. As hard as it is to believe, they often don't understand their own motivations. More often than not, the persons believe themselves to be doing God a favor. They see themselves as the protectors of the church. Consider Paul, who dragged Christians before the magistrates to be beaten, all in the name of God. Like Paul, religious people are forever persecuting the move of God, thinking they are doing God a favor. For me, this is a very sobering reality. It is one that makes me cry out for God's mercy, lest I also walk in this kind of deception. I want to always walk in His ways, and not try to force Him into my way.

GETTING TO THE *HEART* OF THE MATTER

As the sons of God in the earth, we must understand we will have to carefully walk before the Lord. We must remain humble before Him, allowing the light of His presence to always shine in our hearts. With every spiritual success, we will be even more tempted to think that we know better than those around us do.

Deception can subtly slip into our hearts, eventually blinding us to our condition.

Those who refuse to humble themselves, not allowing divine change to come, will eventually stand in opposition to those who long to walk in His ways. In their opposition, they will think they are doing God a favor. When we see how easy this can happen, we should become extremely serious to guard our heart motivations in order to keep them pure before the Lord. In all actuality, our attitudes concerning those who oppose us can be the very crucible to test our heart motivations.

The heart is a very mysterious part of us. The Bible is clear the heart is not only wicked, it is hard to discern.

The heart is deceitful above all things, and desperately wicked; who can know it? I, the Lord, search the heart, I test the mind, even to give every man according to his ways, according to the fruit of his doings (Jeremiah 17:9-10).

The heart is the part of man that only God can know and truly deal with. Because our motivations and thoughts are so deeply embedded into our soul, it is very difficult to know the heart. As the ancient prophet said, "The heart is very deceitful." Even when we think we know our heart, it can be against us. As we begin to understand this reality, we should be slow to not judge the heart of another, neither should we be confident that we know our own heart. Remember the rule—humble in all things. We should realize the greatest test of the heart is time. That which is within us will be manifested in our actions. When God does uncover a bad heart, then it is time to deal with it. God is committed to creating a clean and pure heart, and therefore, He will shine His light within uncovering those dark crevices of our sinful ways.

JUDGING THE HEART

But with me it is a very small thing that I should be judged by you or by a human court. In fact, I do not even judge myself. For I know of nothing against myself, yet I am not justified by this; but He who judges me is the Lord. Therefore judge nothing before the time, until the Lord comes, who will both bring to light the hidden things of darkness and reveal the counsels of the hearts. Then each one's praise will come from God (1 Corinthians 4:3-5).

God does judge our hearts because He loves us and desires that we be liberated from the darkness within. We need to walk with God in humility and repentance and take advantage of opportunities to deal with the issues of the heart when they arise.

Let no one say when he is tempted, "I am tempted by God"; for God cannot be tempted by evil, nor does He Himself tempt anyone. But each one is tempted when he is drawn away by his own desires and enticed (James 1:13-14).

Sin originates in the heart, which is the seat of all our actions. Often, unfortunately, we do not understand our spiritual weakness until we have sinned. It is then that we realize what is really in our hearts. It is those inward desires, that we are often unaware of, that draw us away from our place with Father. This is why God's Word warns us all to be careful lest we fall.

If one falls, we are called to humbly restore the fallen when they make mistakes. That is why God put us in a family, so that we might be able to cover one another with the grace and mercy of the Lord. Without the grace of God restraining and protecting us, we can become vulnerable. Since our heart is revealed through circumstance, the Church must be a place of restoration and humility in order to bring us to maturity in the ways of God. Sadly, in too many places, judgment triumphs over mercy, and God's people continue to remain unhealed. But how wonderful that in the house of mercy, our hearts can become exposed *and* healed without shame or condemnation.

Therefore let him who thinks he stands take heed lest he fall (1 Corinthians 10:12).

One of the great dangers for all true sons is the temptation of pride. Spiritual deception, if not soon detected and corrected, will lead to a great fall. The evidence that first surfaces is the sin of rebellion, the falling away. The root word, *rebel*, speaks of a separation or divorce. It speaks of a separation from truth. The first falling away that happens is a separation of ourselves from other people. You may be deceived and refuse to listen, but there are people around you who can clearly see the problem and long to help you. You still feel you must separate yourself from this confrontation with the truth. Whenever someone begins to separate, you can be sure a choice has been made to walk in a different way. Like satan in the beginning, you say, "I will go my own way." Like Adam who followed in his steps, you say, "I will go my own way; I will do it my way." You become self-centered, not God centered. But the truth would be easy to see if you would listen to the good, sound voices around you.

A segment of King David's life is a good illustration of this truth. When David had sinned with Bathsheba, he first thought he could justify himself and cover up the problem. Everything was neat and tidy until God sent the prophet to him. To confront David, Nathan used a parable about a rich man who stole from a poor man. When David heard this story, it was easy to determine the right thing to do in that situation. The problem was—he did not see his own circumstances in the story until Nathan actually pointed the finger at him.

FINDING THE TRUTH IN THE COUNSEL OF OTHERS

If we can somehow eliminate our selfish ambition and seek the truth, then that truth becomes easier to see. Taking out personal desires from the equation gives the mind an ability to function more effectively. But because this is difficult to do, the Bible advises that we seek our answers in the multitude of counselors. This is why we must not separate ourselves from the advice of other people. In order to find objectivity, we must seek it outside our own window of reality. When we don't seek counsel, it is the surest sign we want to go our own way. This is why we need voices outside our system from time to time. The voices of another perspective can challenge our personal or even collective patterns of thought. This challenge will stretch us so that together we can find the truth of God. True spiritual sons recognize the need for this prophetic input in their personal life and the life of their church. The sons of God understand that the voice of God often comes from others who are outside our normal systems. It is too easy for us to become "yes" men to our own patterns of thought because we are never challenged by an opposing view. Jesus was the voice outside the system in His day, challenging that system to hear His voice. How sad it is that they did not listen.

THE MANY SIDES OF TRUTH

Remember truth is multifaceted, containing more than one side. In Ephesians 3:10 Paul speaks about the manifold or the "many sided" wisdom of God. The rebellious or the religious person does not want truth; he wants to be right. In that case, there is only one way to see truth—his way. Being right is not walking in truth. It is one-sided. There is a big difference between seeking truth and being right. Being right focuses on your interpretation of reality, and it usually focuses on you. Pride and haughtiness have become the friends of the man who walks in his own light. After all, you are right. This is the "man" side of sin. Oh how sweet to be right! We love to be right and we love to make someone else wrong. This is why whenever a problem or confrontation arises, we seek to blame the person who is wrong. It reenforces our position of being right.

RELIGIOUS PEOPLE WILL *KILL FOR THEIR CAUSE*— JESUS ASKED US TO *DIE FOR HIS CAUSE*

If ever this glaring concept has been manifested, it has been revealed in the religious mind-set of the Muslim extremists of our day. They think they are doing God a favor by killing thousands of innocent people as happened on September 11. This is a religious spirit on a grand scale and the height of religious deception. We must, however, also resist it on a much smaller scale in our personal lives and in the local church.

LETTING GO OF THE OLD SO THAT WE CAN EMBRACE THE NEW

When I was a young person in church, I noted the greatest hindrance to what God wanted to do in my life was self-centered motivation. It is one thing to say we want the church to grow; it is another thing altogether to let something upset us as simple as someone claiming our pew on Sunday morning! Most Christians love to sit in the same comfortable seat week after week. We love our routines and become easily offended when someone interferes with them. We hate it when someone challenges our comfortable place and will likely fight back when they do so.

How much more will we fight if it appears someone is coming to take our place? In a growing church, new talent means shared positions. Often in a small church, one person can be in charge of many areas. But when growth comes, you are confronted with the fact you must give up "positions" if that growth is to continue. Sadly, too many of us attach our identity to what we do in the church; and if we lose our job, we think that we have lost a part of ourselves. Everything about growth speaks of letting go of one thing so that we can accept the new. There simply cannot be forward motion if we do not let go.

When it costs us something personally, it becomes easy to fall into religious opposition and fight the very move of God you had been originally praying for. People don't always see what is happening because it occurs subtly. And before we know it, the church quickly becomes the opposition to the next move of God. Why? Because they are not willing to let go of "yesterday" so that they can embrace "tomorrow."

We think that there is no way that we could have ever stood with the Pharisees in the time of Christ, but church history has proven the opposite to be true. We could have stood with them in proud opposition to this new Voice that came to upset our apple cart. We also could have easily defended our temple and structures. We could have resented the changes He was seeking to implement, just like the people of His day had. Unfortunately, we often are doing exactly the same thing in our day. As the sons of God arise in this day, many others shall stand in opposition, Bibles in hand; but the move of God will go on. His purposes will triumph in the end. So, on which side will you stand?

STANDING FOR THE LEAST AND THE LOST

Jesus came to seek and save the lost, and He identified Himself with the least and the lost among the sons of men. The religious establishment hated the ministry of the Son of God. Although they claimed the same mandate, they resisted every effort Jesus made to reach out to the world. The establishment hated anything that was not centered on them; therefore, Jesus couldn't reach the lost by staying centered in the temple with the established order. When they challenged His preference for the non-religious and disenfranchised, He had a wise response:

> *And when the Pharisees saw it, they said to His disciples, "Why does your Teacher eat with tax collectors and sinners?" When Jesus heard that, He said to them, "Those who are well have no need of a physician, but those who are sick"* (Matthew 9:11-12).

Breaking the self-centered mind-set is not easy, because it is so difficult to separate it from our perceived desire to please God. In the late 1980s, our church had purchased 52 acres of land next to the interstate highway—plenty of land in an ideal location. We developed a plan for a building, which initially would seat 2000 people, with expansion capabilities to accommodate 3000 people. Knowing the mind of God for our growth, this seemed to be a perfect plan. When we took our plans to the local government, however, they didn't agree with us or with our plans. They were not even happy about the thought of us building in their community! During our meeting with them, they said some nasty things about the type of people they thought we would be. I was aroused to righteous indignation. (At least I thought it was righteous indignation. It actually was self-righteous indignation!) God was at work, but it was not immediately apparent in my attitude.

When I went to the Lord to complain about these high-minded sinners, He spoke a word to my heart. It was from the Scriptures found in Romans 13:

> *Let every soul be subject to the governing authorities. For there is no authority except from God, and the authorities that exist*

are appointed by God. Therefore whoever resists the authority resists the ordinance of God, and those who resist will bring judgment on themselves. For rulers are not a terror to good works, but to evil. Do you want to be unafraid of the authority? Do what is good, and you will have praise from the same (Romans 13:1-3).

I couldn't reconcile these verses with what I felt the Lord had given us concerning the vision for the local church. God had given me a vision for a large worship center, as well as instructions about other ministries that we would need to build. To fulfill the vision, we needed all the land. But they not only resisted the size of the church building we were proposing, they also let us know they would oppose our efforts to develop this land according to our vision for the future.

I cried out, "Lord, how can we submit to those who appear in opposition to the vision?" But I knew the Lord had spoken, and the Scriptures were obviously clear on this matter. With this word as our direction, we went back to the government officials and humbly let them direct us in the size and scope of our ministry. The building would have a capacity to seat only 1200 people. We were at two services within three months of our new location. It wasn't what I wanted, but it was what the Lord had in mind. The Lord was going to break a mind-set I had which would have hindered the vision He had given. What I thought was working against me was actually working for me.

GOD OUT OF THE BOX

I was raised in church and had always had a great love for the church, but I had a mind-set of ministry that was different than the one of Jesus Christ. Although the plans of God are church-centered, they are not centered on a building. My idea of ministry had actually been a self-centered one, although I would not have perceived it so. My focus had become obscured by the focus on the building. Like so many good intentioned people, I had put God in my box and was willing to fight for Him if I needed to. The trouble with my plan was that God didn't want to be in the box I had created for

Him. He wanted me to get out of my self-contained arena and reach out for the lost, and like Jesus Christ, go where the sinners were, not just invite the sinners to come to Him. Jesus had multitudes of people who sought Him out but He was always on the move seeking people out as well. Although I saw this as a prison binding me up, it would actually become a door of opportunity.

TURNING PROBLEMS INTO OPPORTUNITES

Because we did not have to expend all our resources for a church building, the Lord was able to direct us in another way. An opportunity to purchase a tennis center opened up to us, and we were able to buy it and turn it into a community center. We had such success that we eventually bought the shopping center I worked at as a young man, in order to build another community center. This community center houses an after-school program for middle-school children and a dance school. Because our new church building was not big enough, we had also kept our old church building, and eventually converted it to a media center, performing arts center, and an outreach church to the growing Hispanic population in our area. We also bought a school building for our school and a house for transitional living. With my old mind-set, I would have built a cumbersome fortress for the people of God. Instead, now we have six cities of refuge where the needs of our community are being effectively met.

The long-term effect—we now have a great rapport with our community. Like Jesus, through serving, we have earned a place at the table of our community. We have cast off our self-serving attitudes and become servants of the Lord to our world. We easily could have gone the way of religion and fought our perceived enemies, but by His grace, we chose to follow the example of Jesus Christ. In love, we died to ourselves so that we could live to serve and minister to the people of our world. We actually minister to thousands of people a year who never step foot in a church. We are meeting the people where they are, and the results are what God wants for His people in the earth. We have become the priests to the people He loves.

But you shall be named the priests of the Lord, they shall call you the servants of our God. You shall eat the riches of the Gentiles, and in their glory you shall boast (Isaiah 61:6).

Our loving service has created a platform from which we can speak to our community. Now we have an opportunity to truly reach the people in the world. Now that we have earned the right to speak, we also have to learn how to speak. Jesus had a forum to speak to the people of His day. His openness to receive and minister to the people gave Him that opportunity. Once you have the forum from which to speak, you have to know how to speak. You have to learn how to reach people where they are and to communicate with them in a way that they can understand and appreciate.

Chapter Eight

A Message of Grace for a Weary World

*For God so loved the world that He gave His only begotten Son, that whoever believes in Him should not perish but have everlasting life. **For God did not send His Son into the world to condemn the world,** but that the world through Him might be saved* (John 3:16-17, emphasis added).

As the sons of God in the world, we need to learn how to approach the world the way Jesus did—from a position of love, not judgment. It was love that created His mission, and it was love that fulfilled that mission to the world. It is only when we walk in the Spirit of Christ that we will be able to have the positive impact on our world as Jesus did on His. Jesus never had a shortage of listeners to His message. The dynamics of His love and the power of His message drew people from every stratum of life. But it was especially the weak and lowly who were drawn to Him. There was something magnetic about Him that attracted people and made people want to reach out to Him. Even when Jesus resisted the people approaching Him, there was something compelling them to press forward. Like the woman with the issue of blood, people knew if they could just get a hold of His garment, they would be made well. By the power of His touch, He drew people into the Father's love and healing power.

Jesus came to the world compelled by His Father's love; He did not come to bring judgment. Why do the messengers of the church seem so compelled to condemn people? Regretfully, the church is known more for her judgmental attitudes than for a loving heart. It is certainly not the Spirit of Christ motivating us to condemn others. In truth, it is our own human flesh, masked in religious arguments, motivating us to bring condemnation to our world rather than the love of Christ. It is hard for us to believe that the grace and mercy of God can really bring change to people. We are more comfortable with exposing their shame as opposed to covering their shame. Grace seems too easy. We think in our minds that we are the ones who have to change people. But this is simply a lack of faith on our part in the work of the cross and the life of Jesus Christ.

RESTORATION OF DAVID'S TABERNACLE

The great harvest of God that we all long to see will not come until we have seen the restoration of David's tabernacle, as proclaimed by the prophet Amos:

> *"On that day I will raise up the tabernacle of David, which has fallen down, and repair its damages; I will raise up its ruins, and rebuild it as in the days of old; that they may possess the remnant of Edom, and all the Gentiles who are called by My name," says the Lord who does this thing. "Behold, the days are coming," says the Lord, "when the plowman shall overtake the reaper, and the treader of grapes him who sows seed; the mountains shall drip with sweet wine, and all the hills shall flow with it"* (Amos 9:11-13).

What is this restoration of the tabernacle of David? We need to go to the Book of Acts, chapter 15 for the answer. In the early Church, there was a great debate as to whether the early Christians needed to follow the law of Moses or not. This conflict came to a head at the Jerusalem council recorded in this chapter. Paul and Barnabas urged the early Church leaders to read the prophecies of old, where they were encouraged to see how these prophecies proclaimed the day when the gospel would go to all the nations of the earth and open a floodgate of joy to those outside the Jewish nation. Paul understood that if they attempted to lay the heavy moral codes on these young believers, it would have a devastating effect upon the cause of Christ. Paul argued from the place of grace and urged the leaders to not lay this heavy yoke on the Gentiles.

The Church accepted this challenge and released the Gentile Church from the law of Moses. People would not be separated from God by laws and religious ritual, but would be able to receive Him by faith. Christ was the door, not Moses.

PITCHING A TENT FOR HIS PRESENCE

This tabernacle concept is a picture drawn from the Old Testament as David pitched a tent for the Ark of the Covenant. The Old Testament tabernacle contained three dimensions: the outer court, inner court, and the Most Holy Place. One had to go through an elaborate ritual to reach God in the Most Holy Place. In fact, only the high priest could enter the Most Holy Place, and this happened only once a year. When the Ark of the Covenant finally made its way to Jerusalem after being returned by the Philistines, David pitched the tent for the ark in his backyard, so to speak, because he wanted to be close to the presence of God. In this bit of history, you can see a picture of God's ideal. God was not *separate* from the people, but immediately available to His people. Ritualism tends to separate us from God, while revival brings us back to God.

When Jesus came to the earth, the presence of God was present in the tabernacle of His flesh. God had come in the presence of Jesus and made Himself immediately available to the people. John says that He came and pitched His tent among us.

In the New Testament, the Church becomes this same tabernacle of God. Now, through the Church, God can dwell among the people, and He becomes available to everyone through His people. What an awesome responsibility and how important it is that we reflect the reality of Father in an accurate way! Any time we deny people access to God by our life or words, we are denying the whole principle of the new covenant. Jesus came to tear down walls and barriers that separated God's people from the presence of His Father.

We not only need to allow people access to God, but we must also recognize He is not sitting in the judgment seat when they come. The writer of Hebrews said, "Therefore let us draw near with confidence to the throne of grace, so that we may receive mercy and find grace to help in time of need" (Heb. 4:16 NASB). Father's throne is constructed with the materials of grace and mercy. When you come to the "Most Holy Place" where the presence of God dwells, you will see Him sitting on the mercy seat. Through the blood of Jesus Christ, God makes Himself available to the world. If they will come to Him, He will bring change to their lives by the power of His grace, love, and mercy. Our mission as the sons of God is to reflect that image to a world starving for just a little taste of that love.

LOVE CASTS OUT FEAR

Love has been perfected among us in this: that we may have boldness in the day of judgment; because as He is, so are we in this world. There is no fear in love; but perfect love casts out fear, because fear involves torment. But he who fears has not been made perfect in love (1 John 4:17-18).

We are called to bring God's perfect love into our world. This love does not operate from a position of fear. Many times we think we can produce righteousness in other people by creating an atmosphere of fear and intimidation. Many times we, as Christians, project an image of an angry people who are at odds with the world instead of an image of loving healers who care for our world. You can't *intimidate* the sinner to a place of righteousness.

So then, my beloved brethren, let every man be swift to hear, slow to speak, slow to wrath; for the wrath of man does not produce the righteousness of God (James 1:19-20).

The "wrath of man" is so opposite the ministry of Jesus Christ. He was with the people, caring for them and loving them to a place of wholeness. He wasn't pointing fingers; He was offering a helping hand. Why are we always blaming people for things? Could it be because we are not spiritual, but carnal? Since the garden, man has been looking to blame others for his circumstances. When sin came into the world, Adam blamed Eve, Eve blamed the serpent, and of course we know, the serpent didn't have a leg to stand on! The church is still continuing this tradition. We all are guilty of playing the blame game. Condemnation and judgment are rampant in the church, and it flows from there into the streets of our cities. We have marred the image of God with our petty finger-pointing; consequently, we have not impacted our world. In fact, the Scripture declares we will not be able to release the power of God in our world until we put away the "pointing of the finger."

Then your light shall break forth like the morning, your healing shall spring forth speedily, and your righteousness shall go before you; the glory of the Lord shall be your rear guard. Then you shall call, and the Lord will answer; you shall cry, and He will say, "Here I am." If you take away the yoke from your midst, the pointing of the finger, and speaking wickedness (Isaiah 58:8-9).

It appears that we are more comfortable with judgment rather than mercy. However, Jesus did not come into the world to judge the world and neither should we. Jesus taught us to understand the Word has its own judgment. In other words, because the laws of God are for our good, we know that whenever a person commits sin, the Word itself is vindicated as the person suffers the consequence of their transgression. Sin breeds its own judgment. Since we know sin doesn't pay and every sin has its just consequence, we should rest from our need to pronounce judgment on others and be content in our joyous proclamation of the good news of the gospel. Jesus came declaring that all men are free as they come to Him. He will set them free from the consequences of their sins and liberate them from the stranglehold of sin.

Of course, we also understand that all people in the end will appear before the judgment seat of Christ. But this judgment is for the end of time, not now.

And if anyone hears My words and does not believe, I do not judge him; for I did not come to judge the world but to save the world. He who rejects Me, and does not receive My words, has that which judges him—the word that I have spoken will judge him in the last day (John 12:47-48).

There will be a time Jesus will sit in the seat of judgment. It is also declared in the Word that we will do the same. In the meantime, we are to sit in the seat of mercy.

HIS YOKE IS EASY; HIS BURDEN IS LIGHT

Since my childhood, I have found that the Word of God works. Walking in the principles of the Word will always bring good success. Truly the way of the transgressor is hard, but Jesus said His yoke is easy and His burden light. Sin will bring its own judgment. If it doesn't fully happen in this world, it will certainly happen in the one to come. Yet, the purpose for the Church is not to be sin monitors in our world. Likewise, it is not our job to speak of God's judgment. Although we have done much of this in the past, the Scriptures declare the message of the Church to be the message of "good news." We need to begin to preach the real gospel—a gospel declaring to people that a loving Savior has appeared not to increase their guilt, but to free them from their guilt. He has come to heal their shame, not expose their shame.

The gospel of Jesus Christ has four components: proclamation of the end of the battle and peace with God; good tidings of the benefits of the cross; the truth of salvation; and the announcement that our God reigns.

> *How beautiful upon the mountains are the feet of him who brings good news, who **proclaims peace**, who **brings glad tidings of good things**, who **proclaims salvation**, who **says to Zion, "Your God reigns!"*** (Isaiah 52:7, emphasis added)

How can we proclaim peace when we are constantly picking a fight with the world? How can we bring the good news when for most Christians bad news is more exciting? Ever notice that for most preachers, bad news is more interesting than good news because it gives them something to preach about on Sunday morning? Too many preachers just love preaching on "hell, fire, and brimstone." Finally, how can we preach the reign of God when we seem to think the world is out of control and satan is all-powerful? I believe the Church has a lot of repenting to do for the false messages that we have proclaimed. We need a "change of mind" that will put us in sync with God instead of being preoccupied with the religious mind-sets that put us in opposition to God and in discord with His Word.

THE LIGHT OF HIS GLORY

Isaiah, the prophet, declared that darkness would cover the earth, and gross darkness the people. Yet, we are not called to focus on the darkness, but to preach about the Light. He says when this comes about, we need to arise and shine and let the glory of God be seen upon us. What is the glory of the Lord? When Moses asked God to see His glory, He responded:

*And he said, "Please, show me Your glory." Then He said, "I will make **all My goodness** pass before you, and I will proclaim the name of the Lord before you. I will be gracious to whom I will be gracious, and I will have compassion on whom I will have compassion"* (Exodus 33:18-19, emphasis added).

When darkness comes into our life, our human response is to fight back with threats, accusations, and warnings of impending judgment. But fighting the darkness will not make it go away. God says let the glory of who He is come forth. The only way to dispel the darkness is to "turn on the light of His glory." Let the world see the bright lights of the compassion and graciousness of God. This will contrast greatly with the darkness they are living in and give them something to run to.

While facing the opposition of the religious establishment, Jesus found favor with the secular society. Isn't that amazing! If we want to go and seek the lost, we must seek them in the same manner Jesus did. Our relationship with secular society is not based upon confronting their sins from a self-righteous position but upon a glorious presentation of His compassion and His Kingdom message. This is the reason why the Church has had such a small impact on the world in which we live. Our manner is wrong and our message is wrong. Whenever Jesus addressed the issue of sin, He did so in the context of those who were claiming themselves to be the children of God. But when it came to the world, His message was one of freedom, love, and mercy.

PROCLAIMING FATHER'S MERCY

Have you ever noticed how many preachers and Christians are always talking about the sin in the world? Since I have been a child,

I have heard God's judgment being proclaimed by preachers upon the sin of our nation. But our rush to judgment has not been in the Spirit of Christ. I am 48 years old, which is not a long time in some circles, but is certainly a fair amount of time to say that the Church has been preaching judgment. It has been the predominant theme in the pulpit and on the streets. And where has all the judgment the Church has proclaimed taken us? Perhaps God's mercy lasts a little longer than ours does. Remember when Peter asked Jesus how many times he should forgive; Jesus' response was, "Seventy times seven." I think the Church has not yet exhausted the loving forgiveness of the Father.

A Covenant of Peace

The only time God sent great judgment upon the earth was in the days of the flood of Noah. The Word declares that this event was a sad thing for God and that He determined not to repeat this action.

> *"For this is like the waters of Noah to Me; for as I have sworn that the waters of Noah would no longer cover the earth, so have I sworn that I would not be angry with you, nor rebuke you. For the mountains shall depart and the hills be removed, but My kindness shall not depart from you, nor shall My covenant of peace be removed," says the Lord, who has mercy on you* (Isaiah 54:9-10).

Were you aware God has made a covenant of peace with the earth? This is what the rainbow should represent to us. It is God promising hope for the Messiah who would come and indeed bear the sin of the world. Jesus paid the price for sin. Why are we minimizing the greatness of His sacrifice? Instead of making small His sacrifice, we should be doing the one thing that the Scriptures tell us made the cross worthwhile. We should be seeking for the godly seed, the divine offspring of Christ, in the earth.

> *Yet it pleased the Lord to bruise Him; He has put Him to grief. When You make His soul an offering for sin, He shall see His seed, He shall prolong His days, and the pleasure of the Lord shall prosper in His hand. He shall see the labor of His*

soul, and be satisfied. By His knowledge My righteous Servant shall justify many, for He shall bear their iniquities (Isaiah 53:10-11).

On Sept 11, 2001, terrorists attacked the United States. It was a despicble act of terror and evil. And what was the response of the religious establishment? The first thing many of the religious establishment said was that it was judgment falling upon America because of her sins. Even many of the ones who didn't say it were thinking it. A few well-known leaders, when admonished regarding their stance on this issue, backed down on their statements, but their comments that followed indicated it was a matter of expedience rather than conviction. From a heavenly perspective, the problem with sinners is not that they sin. Sinning is what sinners do. From Heaven's perspective what is needed is a messenger who will tell them about the gospel—the good news of the gospel declaring how much Jesus loves them and how He died for their sins. *We are not supposed to point the finger at the world but point our fingers at Jesus Christ, who is the Savior of the world.* We need to preach the good news of the gospel. Isaiah chapter 61 must be our message. It is a promise of hope, deliverance, comfort, and joy. How could someone turn that down? Yet, instead of preaching and demonstrating the message of Jesus Christ, the firstborn Son, we stand around pointing the finger and speaking of divine judgment. If God sends judgment upon a country, it will be because the Church has not done her part in being salt and light to the country.

IF MY PEOPLE...

If My people who are called by My name will humble themselves, and pray and seek My face, and turn from their wicked ways, then I will hear from heaven, and will forgive their sin and heal their land (2 Chronicles 7:14).

Note it says, "If My people." Why are we always concerning ourselves with what sinners are doing when it is the Church God is speaking to? Remember the story of Sodom and Gomorrah. When Abraham heard the Lord's announcement of His impending judgment upon the city of Sodom, he made intercession for the city, and

God heard His cry. All Abraham had to do was come up with ten righteous people and the city would have been saved. Unfortunately, he obviously could not do that, and both cities, Sodom and Gomorrah, were destroyed. It is interesting to note in the Scriptures that the nephew of Abraham, Lot, lived in Sodom. The Bible tells us that Lot was vexed by the filthy conversation of the wicked. God delivered him out of that city, but how sad that he had had such little influence there. This is the condition of the Church today. We sit around being vexed and condemning the secular society when God wants us to be intercessors like Abraham and, of course, Jesus Christ. God wants us as intercessors to have power with God and learn to exercise it before the people. God wants His love letters to be written on the fabric of our lives so that they can be clearly read by all those who pass by our lives.

A Heart and a Word

Once we have the heart God wants us to have, then it is necessary to understand how we can convey the message to the world in which we live. Jesus Himself gave us the example. Jesus conveyed the message by living and interacting with the people. His was a message lived before the people. Jesus did this by being a normal and natural part of His environment. Jesus was not too religious to hang out with the people of His day. He loved being with the sinners and the tax collectors. The Gospel of Luke, chapter 19 gives an example of this. Jesus had an encounter with a man by the name of Zacchaeus. Zach was rich and he was also a tax collector, so he had two strikes against him. The religious people of Jesus' day hated the tax collectors. (Of course, we are not very fond of them in our own day.) When Jesus came to town, Zach was so excited to see Him that he climbed up into a tree just to make sure that he at least got a glimpse. When Jesus saw him, He told him to come down because He had decided that He was going to his house for dinner. The religious people complained because Jesus was spending too much time with a sinner. Jesus responded this way:

And Jesus said to him, "Today salvation has come to this
house, because he also is a son of Abraham; for the Son of

118

Man has come to seek and to save that which was lost" (Luke 19:9-10).

LOOKING FOR THE HURTING ONES

We can't save the lost if we are not out seeking them. The Son of God went outside the comfort zones of the assembly in order to seek out the lost. As I mentioned, God led us as a local church in a way we did not expect. Although I once had a building-complex mind-set, through the work of the Holy Spirit, I was able to realize God wanted us to have a community and people-centered mind-set.

Our local church has established two centers in our area where we minister to our community. We offer them things they like to do. We have over 100,000 square feet of recreation space available. We offer basketball, a roller-blade rink, roller-blade and skateboard jumps, a dance school, and a kid's playroom. You name it; we probably have it. We not only want to offer recreation, but we also want to teach proper boundaries in those things. For instance, we have a dance school with over 500 enrollments. It stands in contrast to the secular schools where the girls are taught sensuality and not the art of dance. We even have dances in our club for young adults and teens, which are free from an environment of alcohol and smoking. We've had our share of unkind comments from the religious folk. Never mind that when the prodigal son came home, there was the sound of music and dancing. Stop! Don't put the book down now! Come out of your comfort zone and let God make you more like Jesus and less like the Pharisees. We have to be controversial to get where God is taking us today and that means bucking the system. We must confront true sin, yet at the same time teach discernment and personal responsibility to the people.

LEARNING TO DISCERN
BETWEEN THE HOLY AND THE PROFANE

And they shall teach My people the difference between the holy and the unholy, and cause them to discern between the unclean and the clean. In controversy they shall stand as judges, and judge it according to My judgments. They shall keep

My laws and My statutes in all My appointed meetings, and they shall hallow My Sabbaths (Ezekiel 44:23-24).

In the church today, we have people who disassociate themselves from everything in the world; and on the other hand, we have people who easily join in with the entertainment of the day without questioning the limits necessary to maintain the integrity of their spiritual walk. Jesus was obviously someone who was involved and participated in His world; we can also be sure He would have exercised discernment about what was good and edifying. The religious leaders persecuted Him for this. Jesus was exasperated by the comments of the religious establishment and declared:

For John came neither eating nor drinking, and they say, "He has a demon." The Son of Man came eating and drinking, and they say, "Look, a glutton and a winebibber, a friend of tax collectors and sinners!" But wisdom is justified by her children (Matthew 11:18-19).

Jesus was a person who could meet the people where they were and set an example of righteousness for them, not a righteousness of flesh, but the true righteousness of God. It's time to take off our religious clothing and be clothed with the righteousness of Christ! This righteousness will be the light to attract the world to the cause of Christ. This is a righteousness the world can relate to. This is not the self-righteousness of a religious people who are more concerned about comparing righteousness with other Christians than conveying the message of Christ to their generation. This is the true righteousness God wants to reveal to the world in which we live. Once we get in contact with these people, we must recognize our job is to bring them to God so He can change them. We must do our part, but also let God do His part. This fulfills the prophecy of the prophet, Amos, and will open the door for the greatest harvest of all times.

Chapter Nine

Will You Trust Him?—
The Just Will Live by Faith

For the law of the Spirit of life in Christ Jesus has made me free from the law of sin and death (Romans 8:2).

In order for the Church to become true spiritual sons, we have to understand what it means to live in the Spirit of life in Christ. It is by the Spirit that we are made free from the law of sin and death. When the first Adam sinned, death came into the world. Jesus, the last Adam, came not only to give us forgiveness of sin, but also to deliver us from the power and the curse of sin.

And she will bring forth a Son, and you shall call His name Jesus, for He will save His people from their sins (Matthew 1:21).

To move into the spiritual dimensions that God wants us to live in during these days, we must walk fully in the new covenant God has made with us. When Jesus came into the world, He came to the Jewish people. He came as their Messiah.

But He answered and said, "I was not sent except to the lost sheep of the house of Israel" (Matthew 15:24).

When the house of Israel rejected Him, the gospel then was released to all the nations of the world just as God had planned from the very beginning.

I say then, have they stumbled that they should fall? Certainly not! But through their fall, to provoke them to jealousy, salvation has come to the Gentiles (Romans 11:11).

121

Even us whom He called, not of the Jews only, but also of the Gentiles? As He says also in Hosea: "I will call them My people, who were not My people, and her beloved, who was not beloved" (Romans 9:24-25).

GOD'S NEW COVENANT WITH MAN

Throughout the generations, people have been trying to synthesize the old and new covenants together. The result of such efforts ends up in a gritty mixture. God didn't tell the people of Israel He was going to fix the first covenant; He promised to make a new covenant.

Behold, the days are coming, says the Lord, when I will make a new covenant with the house of Israel and with the house of Judah—not according to the covenant that I made with their fathers in the day that I took them by the hand to lead them out of the land of Egypt, My covenant which they broke, though I was a husband to them, says the Lord (Jeremiah 31:31-32).

This new covenant would be of the heart and not of the law.

But this is the covenant that I will make with the house of Israel after those days, says the Lord: I will put My law in their minds, and write it on their hearts; and I will be their God, and they shall be My people (Jeremiah 31:33).

The law of Moses had a threefold impact on Israel. First, it was the governing contract between God and the house of Israel that created the structure for their behavior in the land of promise. It was the law for the land. In this sense the law was for the Jew. It is called the law of Moses, from this point of view, not the law of God. It was the constitution and bylaws for the nation of Israel.

Next, the law of Moses was a prophetic document. For those who could look through the prophetic lens, they could see beyond the legal structure of the law. They could see the prophetic fingerprints of the coming Messiah. The law pointed forward to a time when Messiah would come and fulfill all that was contained in its words.

Philip found Nathanael and said to him, "We have found Him of whom Moses in the law, and also the prophets, wrote—Jesus of Nazareth, the son of Joseph" (John 1:45).

Through the types and shadows of the Old Testament law and ordinances, we see a pattern of the heavenly things. It is through these heavenly things that we see a picture of the Christ.

For if He were on earth, He would not be a priest, since there are priests who offer the gifts according to the law; who serve the copy and shadow of the heavenly things, as Moses was divinely instructed when he was about to make the tabernacle. For He said, "See that you make all things according to the pattern shown you on the mountain" (Hebrews 8:4-5).

Finally, the law came to make people conscious of the power and consequences of sin. The law made visible the world of sin that was in the heart of man. It identified and magnified man's transgressions.

Therefore, just as through one man sin entered the world, and death through sin, and thus death spread to all men, because all sinned—For until the law sin was in the world, but sin is not imputed when there is no law (Romans 5:12-13).

A PARADIGM SHIFT TOWARDS THE SPIRIT

Jesus came into the world with great compassion to free man from the entanglements of the law. He would do this by introducing a new covenant. Under this new covenant, the law would not be written in rock tablets but would be engraved into the fabric of man's spirit. A great shift now takes place as man moves his focus away from the *letter* of the law to the *Spirit* of the law. Rather than focusing on legalistically adhering to every little commandment, a true spiritual son now focuses on the Spirit, who will empower Him with a new life—a life that comes with power. We need to come out of the legalist mind-set to the mind-set of faith.

When Jesus came, He preached the message of the heart. He was more concerned with the heart attitudes than the outward actions of the people. The prophets had already introduced the need to examine one's heart and not just one's actions, and the Jewish nation had come under the curse of spiritual blindness, because they did not have the religion of the heart. God wanted their hearts. Jesus knew that all action flowed from the heart. If the heart were not changed, then the actions of life would not change.

All life flows from the interior recesses of the inward life, known as the heart.

The religious establishment could not comprehend this message. They were locked into a paradigm and just could not make the transition that would take them out of walking by the letter to walking by the Spirit. Because of their unwillingness to accept this paradigm shift, they rejected Christ and His message and missed out on the great blessing of God.

As an emphasis on the heart issue, one day Jesus told the Jewish crowds, "If you break the law, 'You should not commit adultery' by committing adultery in your heart, you're just as guilty as if you had literally committed adultery." Jesus now raised the moral bar higher than any Jew could jump by introducing the concept that God was more concerned about the heart. He brought them to the place where they could not keep the law through discipline alone. They would need God. The righteousness of man's attempts to keep the law will never satisfy the demands of the Holy God.

But Israel, pursuing the law of righteousness, has not attained to the law of righteousness. Why? Because they did not seek it by faith, but as it were, by the works of the law. For they stumbled at that stumbling stone (Romans 9:31-32).

THE FAITH OF ABRAHAM

This *religion of the heart* would now demand a new level of faith. Get ready! Another spiritual shift is about to happen. We must now move away from the mental adherence to the law. There are those who still think of the law as the foundation of the church. This is a false concept that leads us to much error. The foundation of the church is not the law of Moses, but the life of faith introduced through Abraham. Before there was Moses, there was Abraham. He is the father of us all. The Scriptures declare the gospel was first preached to Abraham even before there was the law.

> *Therefore know that only those who are of faith are sons of Abraham. And the Scripture, foreseeing that God would justify the Gentiles by faith, preached the gospel to Abraham beforehand, saying, "In you all the nations shall be blessed." So then those who are of faith are blessed with believing Abraham* (Galatians 3:7-9).

Abraham embraced the walk of faith. It is this walk of faith that establishes the dynamics of our Christian experience. Look at the power of the walk of faith demonstrated in that one single life. God told Abraham his name would be great. When you consider that Christians, Jews, and Muslims all trace their lineage to Abraham, we can certainly see how that prophecy came to pass. Literally billions claim a heritage through him. Think how great an impact the world will experience, as a generation of believers learns what it means to truly walk in faith! I know that there are many books on faith and we all have heard lots of sermons about faith, but the real issue is not what we know, but how we live. The Father will teach His sons how to relate to Him from the realm of faith.

Today, we can compare ourselves to Abraham when he had two sons. One was of the flesh and the other was of promise. There was a conflict between these two sons and also between the mothers. A time came when Abraham had to get rid of the mixture and walk by faith alone. The bondwoman and her son had to leave. He had to make a commitment to that which originated out of his flesh and that which was born of the Spirit.

> *But, as he who was born according to the flesh then persecuted him who was born according to the Spirit, even so it is now. Nevertheless what does the Scripture say? "Cast out the bondwoman and her son, for the son of the bondwoman shall not be heir with the son of the freewoman"* (Galatians 4:29-30).

Jesus was in continual conflict with the religious crowd. They could not receive His words, because they didn't have the heart for them. Their pride in their own works made them the enemy of God.

So who could receive His message? Those who had no confidence in themselves reached out to embrace Him.

THE LIBERTY OF THE SPIRIT

I remember when I was growing up in church, people were told that they were saved by grace. But in practice our actions did not match our words. There had been such an emphasis on good works that I remember wondering why people who lived clean lives weren't Christians? They're so close. The reason I thought that way was because I had come to think Christianity was a lifestyle of good living, not a walk of faith. My legalistic mind-set thought that since they weren't having fun anyway, they might as well go to church so they could go to Heaven. People with religious mind-sets think Christianity is about suffering now so we can celebrate later. Sinners on the other hand celebrate now and will suffer later. During that time, faith was something I experienced once, when I received Christ, but was certainly not a lifestyle of living. Faith was more a concept than a reality.

It is from this basic mind-set that much of the church still operates. This is why we have churches filled with religious people but not churches filled with people of faith. Remember, God wants us to live by faith.

For in it the righteousness of God is revealed from faith to faith; as it is written, "The just shall live by faith" (Romans 1:17).

This mind-set will change our attitude towards God and also how we deal with others. We will begin to realize we are not under bondage, nor will we force others into bondage.

For you did not receive the spirit of bondage again to fear, but you received the Spirit of adoption by whom we cry out, "Abba, Father." The Spirit Himself bears witness with our spirit that we are children of God (Romans 8:15-16).

We will bring ourselves into the glorious liberty of being the sons of God.

Because the creation itself also will be delivered from the bondage of corruption into the glorious liberty of the children of God (Romans 8:21).

To become the mature sons of God, we must be a people who walk in the liberty of the Spirit of life in Christ. This is the liberty that will bring us into the image of Christ and allow us to fulfill our destiny in Him.

Nevertheless when one turns to the Lord, the veil is taken away. Now the Lord is the Spirit; and where the Spirit of the Lord is, there is liberty. But we all, with unveiled face, beholding as in a mirror the glory of the Lord, are being transformed into the same image from glory to glory, just as by the Spirit of the Lord (2 Corinthians 3:16-18).

When I first received the Holy Spirit in a Pentecostal church, I remember how we loved this verse that spoke about our liberty in the Spirit. To us this meant that if the Holy Spirit was present, we couldn't stop anybody from doing whatever he or she felt like doing in the service. This was during what was called the "Jesus People Movement," and our church was filled with young, and often foolish, kids. When we got going, there were kids literally doing cartwheels down the aisles of the church. The pastor would say, "Loren, I feel like running; run for me!" And off I went running down the aisle. I don't know why I had to run when the pastor felt like running, but I enjoyed myself immensely! We had liberty to do what we wanted to do in the church service, but we certainly didn't have the true liberty of God spoken of in the Scriptures. Now, I understand that the liberty God offers is the liberty to become the person God wants me to be.

WALKING BY FAITH CAN BE A MESSY AFFAIR

Going through the process of being conformed to the image of Christ is a messy affair. I have found that we don't usually rely on God's strength until we run out of our own. Like Abraham, we usually make an Ishmael before we produce an Isaac. Like Jacob, we live as a con man before we can live as an Israel. Like David, we don't know we are shaped in iniquity and sin until we make a terrible mistake as he did with Bathsheba. Like Elijah, when we should be confident in what God has done, we find ourselves sitting in a cave feeling sorry for ourselves. Like the prodigal, we don't know how good it is in the Father's house until we're eating dinner with the pigs. Like Peter, we don't know what we're really made of until we cuss out a little girl and deny we know Christ. As great as all these people became in the purposes of God, they would have been set aside in the average church of our day because they had failed at one point or another in their life. It is time for the freedom produced by grace to come to the house of God.

Does this mean we shouldn't care if we sin? Paul had to answer the same question.

> *What shall we say then? Shall we continue in sin that grace may abound? Certainly not! How shall we who died to sin live any longer in it?* (Romans 6:1-2)

The end result should be deliverance from sin. It must begin, however, by faith. Once we are established in faith, we need His grace to get us through. With grace we can pursue the righteousness of Christ. We must take our focus off each other and place it on the Lord. In this freedom, we must set our sights on Christ. Paul spoke of this in Romans 8 when he said:

> *There is therefore now no condemnation to those who are in Christ Jesus, who do not walk according to the flesh, but according to the Spirit. For the law of the Spirit of life in Christ Jesus has made me free from the law of sin and death* (Romans 8:1-2).

WALKING BY THE SPIRIT OR WALKING BY THE FLESH

Since our goal is the walk of faith through grace, we must recognize we are free from condemnation. This is a big one. Once you are delivered from that little voice that is always screaming condemnation in your ear, you will be free to hear the other voice that will lead you into the purposes of Father. The blood of Jesus Christ has freed us from the guilt and penalty of sin as well as the screaming voice of condemnation. When we sin, we have an advocate with the

Father. All we must do is be honest and confess our condition. When we do confess our sins to the Father, then the mercy and grace of God frees us from the burden of sin until the change comes to our lives. Again, this is not liberty to sin or to live according to the flesh. If we live according to those motivations, we will suffer death. Allowing grace to free us until the work of God is complete, we live pleasing in His sight. On the other hand, we do not please God when we walk in the flesh.

So then, those who are in the flesh cannot please God (Romans 8:8).

However, we do not suffer His wrath when we fail, if our heart is to please Him. He is a God who looks at the heart. Father does not want anyone to live in an atmosphere of "fearing to fail"; He know this puts too much stress on us. It is His desire that we understand that *failure is never final.* He redeems our failures, transforming them into opportunities of reshaping our lives.

The religious mind-set is not able to receive this walk. It is much easier to live by rules and regulations. It does not understand walking by the Spirit. Jesus was faced with this in the religious people of His day. One day when He and His disciples were walking through a field on the Sabbath, His disciples became hungry and picked some food to eat. The Pharisees pointed the accusing finger at them and said, "How can you violate the Sabbath by picking food to eat?" This was the response of Jesus to them:

But if you had known what this means, "I desire mercy and not sacrifice," you would not have condemned the guiltless (Matthew 12:7).

The religious people were always ready to condemn. Jesus did not come to condemn the world but to save the world. This should be the mind-set of all those who seek to walk in His footsteps. Jesus went on to teach that the law was created for people, not the people for the law.

Then He said to them, "What man is there among you who has one sheep, and if it falls into a pit on the Sabbath, will not lay

129

hold of it and lift it out? Of how much more value then is a man than a sheep? Therefore it is lawful to do good on the Sabbath" (Matthew 12:11-12).

And He said to them, "The Sabbath was made for man, and not man for the Sabbath. Therefore the Son of Man is also Lord of the Sabbath" (Mark 2:27-28).

What an amazing thought. The laws were created for us. Most people have the mind-set that God uses the law as a divine obstacle course to prove those worthy of Heaven. Unfortunately, we fail to see the great blessing His Word was meant to give to us. Our lack of understanding of the love of God makes us grovel as we try to gain His favor. Like children in a family with unloving parents, we try to gain the favor of our Father through competition with one another. Our sibling rivalry causes us to compare our spiritual sacrifices with one another. Like Cain before us, we compare our works with someone else's rather than focus on our own personal walk as before God. In the end, we also may seek to kill someone (even if it is through slander and rejection) to gain God's favor.

THE LETTER KILLS—THE SPIRIT GIVES LIFE

For the Church to move forward, we must begin to walk with God in the Spirit of the Word rather than the letter. The letter kills, but it is the Spirit that gives us life. All throughout history, religious people have committed murder and thought they were doing God a favor.

Another illustration of this truth is related in the story of the woman caught in the act of adultery. The men of the city brought her before the Lord Jesus and asked what they should do about this sin. Actually, they were seeking to entrap Him. They wanted Him to deny the law of Moses. Yet, Jesus turned the tables on them. He first knelt and wrote something on the ground. Many a sermon has been written on this subject. What did He write on the ground? It isn't what He wrote that was important; it was why He wrote it. He wanted the men to have time to remove themselves from their emotional reaction motivated by wrong religious thinking and get in touch with their conscience. Then He planted the Word, "Let the one who is without sin cast the first stone." One by one they walked away, because they saw the foolishness of their way. The person who walks in the Spirit must have a soft heart so that God's voice can penetrate into their hearing processes.

While it is said: "Today, if you will hear His voice, do not harden your hearts as in the rebellion" (Hebrews 3:15).

Once we understand that God means well for us and His laws are for our good, any difficulty we face in pleasing Him will not cause us to give up, because we think we cannot measure up. We then can truly walk in the mercy and love God wants us to walk in towards one another. But we cannot show grace and mercy to others until we have first received it for ourselves.

THE RIGHTEOUSNESS PRODUCED BY FAITH

What will produce the true righteousness of God once we have committed ourselves to the walk of faith? It will be the same process God worked in the life of Father Abraham.

Abraham believed God, and it was accounted to him for righteousness. What God says you are is more important than what others are saying about you. Once Abraham's belief was accounted as righteous, he was able to walk with God in a manner that brought great change in his life. God's declaration over his life empowered him for the journey. Every man and woman needs to hear God's declaration over their life.

Abraham's testimony is not just of a man who received a promise and fulfillment from God; it is also a testimony of a changed life. It is a testimony experienced by his wife as well. Both of them found the walk of faith to be a life-changing experience. Concerning Abraham, He said:

No longer shall your name be called Abram, but your name shall be Abraham; for I have made you a father of many nations (Genesis 17:5).

Concerning Sarah He said:

Then God said to Abraham, "As for Sarai your wife, you shall not call her name Sarai, but Sarah shall be her name" (Genesis 17:15).

While the religious mind-set fights over laws and regulations, the Spirit of God cries out for the new creation.

For in Christ Jesus neither circumcision nor uncircumcision avails anything, but a new creation. And as many as walk according to this rule, peace and mercy be upon them, and upon the Israel of God (Galatians 6:15-16).

SEEING AND ENTERING THE KINGDOM

For the evangelical Church, our concept of the new creation is centered in the experience of the new birth. I am sure by your own personal experience you can relate to the dynamic change of outlook that came to you as a result of being born again. The new birth is transference moving us into the realm of Spirit so that we can live in the dimension of God. Without the new birth, you cannot see nor can you enter into the Kingdom of God.

Jesus answered and said to him, "Most assuredly, I say to you, unless one is born again, he cannot see the kingdom of God" (John 3:3).

We need to understand, however, seeing is not entering. Just because you understand a truth does not mean that you have experienced the reality of that truth. Once we can see the Kingdom, once we have experienced the change of outlook that comes from the new birth, God wants us to enter the fullness of His Kingdom so that we can experience all its blessings and power. God is calling the Church to a higher place in Him. This is the time and the season. With Abraham, there was a time God came to him with a greater expectation, a time when He expected Abraham to live the life as a mature son of God.

When Abram was ninety-nine years old, the Lord appeared to Abram and said to him, "I am Almighty God; walk before Me and be blameless. And I will make My covenant between Me and you, and will multiply you exceedingly" (Genesis 17:1-2).

God had already established His covenant with Abraham. Yet now, the process of the "multiplying seed" would confirm the covenant. Now, He could bring forth the righteous seed upon the earth, the same desire God had from the beginning for mankind. God has always wanted a fruitful people who would multiply, fill up the earth, and take dominion. He wanted a people created in His image. Now Abraham and Sarah would be able to receive a new name and a new inheritance. It is this same blessing God wants for the Church today. It is this blessing God says you are ready for. This is the reason you are reading this message right now. Will you receive this Word? Once we hear, we need to understand this experience comes through a *walk* of faith, not just a one-time experience of faith. The call of the new covenant is a call to a life of faith.

> *For I am not ashamed of the gospel of Christ, for it is the power of God to salvation for everyone who believes, for the Jew first and also for the Greek. For in it the righteousness of God is revealed from faith to faith; as it is written, "The just shall live by faith"* (Romans 1:16-17, emphasis added).

What were the stages of this process in the life of Abraham?

THE WALK OF FAITH

In his first encounter with God recorded in Genesis 12, Abraham received the call to the walk of faith. He was called to leave his familiar surroundings and life, to travel to a new life and land the Lord would show him. This was not an easy decision.

When he arrived in the land, the Lord appeared to him, and he built an altar to the God who had made a promise to him and fulfilled the promise by bringing him to the land. Abraham had such faith in this dimension that when a struggle ensued between his servants and the servants of Lot, Abraham was willing to split up with Lot, giving him the first choice of what land he wanted. His trust was in the Lord.

After this, Abraham lifted his eyes and saw by the Spirit the land of his inheritance. This was his first dimension of faith, and it speaks of our initial walk with God as well. Once we begin to walk by faith, then we will begin to see things that we have never seen before. Spiritual vision is for those who have learned to walk by faith.

Abraham was motivated through faith to walk in obedience by leaving his former life and following God. He also showed his obedience of faith through tithing as recorded in Genesis 14. Most people think of tithing as just an issue of obedience, when in fact it is more an issue of faith. Abraham could tithe because he trusted that God was able to take care of him. He knew God was the source.

In Genesis chapter 15, Abraham received an enlargement of his faith. God came to him and revealed Himself as the God who rewards.

After these things the word of the Lord came to Abram in a vision, saying, "Do not be afraid, Abram. I am your shield, your exceedingly great reward" (Genesis 15:1).

Remember, faith comes through hearing the Word of God. We need to have an ear to hear. Our spiritual birth into Father's world gives us the ability to not only see, but also to hear. Seeing and hearing are key elements for those sons who desire to walk by faith.

So then faith comes by hearing, and hearing by the word of God (Romans 10:17).

The faith walk is a walk of growth. It must challenge us to move forward, to enter into new dimensions of spiritual reality. The by-product of this walk will also produce a greater revelation of who God is. It is ultimately this revelation of who God is that produces the faith to become what God wants us to be. It is what we see in God that produces the real change in us. We walk by the power of the things that we have seen.

Beloved, now we are children of God; and it has not yet been revealed what we shall be, but we know that when He is revealed, we shall be like Him, for we shall see Him as He is (1 John 3:2).

Each step of change in us then creates a greater capacity to see more of God. It is this cycle of revelation and faith that produces the mature Christian God has called us to be.

The charismatic Pentecostal experience increases our vision and expectation for supernatural supply from God. Many sincere Christians find it offensive that people look to a God who "supplies all their needs according to His riches." Yet God made the choice to lead us by faith into a great experience in life and also a great experience in Him. Father loves to give to His sons and has great reservoirs of wealth stored up for us.

LETTING GO OF "ISHMAEL"

In this dimension of faith, although Abraham had an enlargement in his understanding of God, it was also the time of his greatest mistakes. Those who walk by faith will stumble from time to time in their spiritual journey. But a true son is never overwhelmed by the failure. He simply gets up, dusts himself off, and keeps moving forward.

In his anxiety about the promise, Abraham gave birth to Ishmael. It was an important lesson in his journey. Once he was willing to deal with his flesh and let Ishmael go, God could increase him for the blessing that would come through Isaac. Many of you reading this book need to hear the call from God to move to this higher dimension in God. Before you can move forward, you need to let "Ishmael" go!

What is "Ishmael"? "Ishmael" is anything born of flesh works and flesh plans, whatever is of the world and not of God. Unfortunately, some of those "Ishmaels" are your efforts to please God or fulfill what you thought was God's purpose for you. Some of our worldly concepts are embodied in religious or spiritual garb. They can be recognized by the test mentioned in Matthew 4 (see Chapter Four of this book). Are they born of faith from the Word? Are they of pride and self-promotion? Are they born of your desire or God's?

Unfortunately, this describes many of our religious organizations, not just our individual plans. It is time to commit yourself to the life of faith. It is time for your greatest level of faith, but also your greatest level of reward and personal satisfaction. To take the next step forward and experience the favor of Father, you will have to discover what is your "Ishmael" and simply let it go.

I WILL MULTIPLY YOU

In Genesis chapter 17, God once again came to Abraham. This would be the time when Abraham would be transformed by the power of God. He would truly become the new creature able to produce the Father's purpose in the earth. What produced this final change in Abraham? It was through the experience of a greater revelation of Father.

> *When Abram was ninety-nine years old, the Lord appeared to Abram and said to him, "I am Almighty God; walk before Me and be blameless. And I will make My covenant between Me and you, and will multiply you exceedingly"* (Genesis 17:1-2).

The walk of faith will produce experiences in God that give us a clearer perception of Him and a greater change in us. The things you see and hear will impact the inward places in your heart and give birth to brand-new spiritual desires. What God does in us He wants to multiply through us! As God's image is being reflected through us, it will bring great glory to Father as well as increase His favor upon us.

> *But we all, with unveiled face, beholding as in a mirror the glory of the Lord, are being transformed into the same image from glory to glory, just as by the Spirit of the Lord* (2 Corinthians 3:18).

Chapter Ten

Breaking the Religious Subculture

For as many as are led by the Spirit of God, these are sons of God (Romans 8:14).

For the law of the Spirit of life in Christ Jesus has made me free from the law of sin and death (Romans 8:2).

God has not called us to be under the law of man, but to walk according to the law of the Spirit. In other words, our lives should not be guided by a set of rules but by the Spirit who lives within us. When you were younger, you were immature and had to be guided by a set of rules and regulations; but if you have grown up, you should be able to function effectively and successfully without those rules and regulations. The reason you no longer need them is because they have been indelibly written on the parchment of your soul.

> *Now I say that the heir, as long as he is a child, does not differ at all from a slave, though he is master of all, but is under guardians and stewards until the time appointed by the father* (Galatians 4:1-2).

When you become mature, you are no longer under the house rules of your parents. You are now a responsible adult and able to make decisions based upon wisdom, knowledge, and experience. The religious system reacts against this concept, because it threatens the control they have over people. *Walking by the Spirit* threatens the hierarchy that so frequently surrounds human organizations that unfortunately give more honor and respect to men than God. Jesus found this to be the case when He came to earth. He was a threat to the system; hence, He became the enemy of the leaders of the system.

*If we let Him go on like this, everyone will believe in Him, and the Romans will come and take away both our **place** and our **nation*** (John 11:48 NIV, emphasis added).

STANDING AGAINST THE FLOW

These leaders did not like the shift moving away from them and were afraid that they would lose their place and the system that supported their place. Often in church history, when God moved in a fresh way, the people flowing with the move of God found themselves at odds with the leadership. Every new move of God has always been a threat to the preceding one.

You cannot learn to be led by the Spirit if you are not first freed from rules and regulations. The person who chooses to live under rules and regulations is not taught to think for himself or taught how to listen to the Holy Spirit. The problem, of course, is not just the leadership. People have a natural inclination towards group conformity. As humans we tend to move in herds because there is safety in remaining in the anonymity of the herd. Thus, it is a normal characteristic of human behavior to develop cultural institutions as the center and focus of our activity.

Since time began, man has developed a culture around clans and villages. But this tendency towards group conformity often stands in opposition to the walk of the Spirit that God wants for us. When God speaks a word to us that is in opposition to the prevailing wind of our culture (religious or secular), most of us are not inclined to threaten our security or our popularity by boldly declaring that word. But we must be willing to step out if we are going to grow up into true sons of the Father.

CULTURE AND RELIGION

When Jesus came to earth, He was a threat to the culture of the religious establishment. A strict religious culture had developed even around the temple. It had once been a house of prayer but over time had become the rallying point for the cultural persuasions of the people. Over the years, these religious leaders had built a fence of more than 600 laws that governed the life of the people of Israel. These rules appeared to be religious, even pious, but in fact were established to protect the culture to which they were accustomed.

Since the time of the Babylonians Israel had been subjugated by other nations. The Romans now held a fist around the neck of the Jewish people. Life in the temple was the only way they could maintain a cultural independence and identity apart from these domineering nations. Much more was involved in the temple activity than simply the desire to please God. The temple had become a cultural center reflecting the religious life that controlled the nation.

The mixing of religion and culture has been very common in the history of man. However, the mixture is not pleasing to God. This is why the most successful Christian church has been the church in the USA. Among modern western societies only the United States of America has maintained a strong church presence and belief in God. The reason for this strength has been the strong separation of the church from the government. Although the church in America has had great influence on the American culture, it is distinct from the system, not a part of it. It is this distinction God intends for the church.

The European nations, which have mixed government and church, have seen a decline in church attendance and belief in God. Unfortunately, today many churches in the United States are likewise building their churches on the basis of American culture. We are being told we have to adopt popular culture if we are to reach the people. The long-term effect of this trend could be disastrous!

Jesus told His disciples they were to be *in* the world but not *of* the world. The church in the USA continues to have a great deal of influence on the culture of the country. The church being separate has strengthened its voice, not hindered it. Whereas in the European tradition, the churches have often been sponsored and supported by the government. The end result is a dead church where the influence on government and society have diminished. The desire for support from the government for the institutional church has drained the church of its power and influence. This is certainly not the pattern one wants to follow. In Latin America, the government and social institutions have protected the church. In doing so, it has become a part of the problem facing the various countries rather than the source of the solution. The church that is under the influence of the government will fall under the judgment of God and will in the end be persecuted by the very source they seek to receive help from.

> *And he cried mightily with a loud voice, saying, "Babylon the great is fallen, is fallen, and has become a dwelling place of demons, a prison for every foul spirit, and a cage for every unclean and hated bird! For all the nations have drunk of the wine of the wrath of her fornication, the kings of the earth have committed fornication with her, and the merchants of the earth have become rich through the abundance of her luxury"* (Revelation 18:2-3).

The Babylonian system is a foreign, humanistic system that operates in contradistinction to all that God is doing. Cultural loyalties within this system are very strong and hard to resist. For many years, the missionary movement was hindered in the spreading of the gospel because missionaries were trying to instill western culture along with the gospel. Imagine Africans in the middle of the jungle taught to wear suits to church services where they had organs for worship but were not allowed to play their drums. Too many of the American missionaries did all of the work, and at the same time, did not allow nationals to ascend into places of responsibility and authority.

Now that the nationals are taking the lead in these countries, the churches are experiencing tremendous growth. The church needs to be very careful in understanding that God has not called us to create a Christian culture but to have a voice and influence on the various cultures of the world. The gospel itself will take its own unique shape within the culture. When Jesus came into the world, He didn't have a problem with the cultural institutions of the time. He endorsed the support of government and actually seemed to flow very well with the social institutions. The religious establishment hated this though, and thought they were pointing out error in His life by observing His participation with popular culture.

> *The Son of Man came eating and drinking, and they say, "Look, a glutton and a winebibber, a friend of tax collectors and sinners!" But wisdom is justified by her children* (Matthew 11:19).

Jesus, obviously, did not have a problem with their accusations. What He did have a problem with was the culture of the religious establishment. Because culture is a natural part of human behavior, it is very common for even religious groups to develop their own cultures. These religious cultures become countercultures to the establishment. You can noticeably observe this concept among people like the Amish and Mennonites in the USA whose culture is so different that it is easily seen in contrast to contemporary society. It is not so evident in less visible religious communities, but their countercultures are often just as real. I have observed that denominations develop their own culture with their own style, lingo, and social order. These cultures are so meticulously observed that someone can go to a church within the same denomination in a different state or country and still feel at home.

Individual churches often do the same thing on a smaller scale. Even informal charismatic fellowships have a tendency to develop a cultural standard through the ordering of their service or by setting standards of dress for the people. These standards need not be officially set; they only have to be observed for a period of time and then people seek to fit the mold of the group. This makes our natural man very comfortable; but is it the desire of God? It is the natural mind operating in a comfortable mode yet resistant to the move of God. It becomes a serious problem when we begin rejecting people because they do not fit or conform to our little religious culture. It becomes an even more serious problem when the Spirit comes in and wants to tear down what we have built because it is in opposition to the Spirit's new direction.

> *For those who live according to the flesh set their minds on the things of the flesh, but those who live according to the Spirit,*

the things of the Spirit. For to be carnally minded is death, but to be spiritually minded is life and peace. Because the carnal mind is enmity against God; for it is not subject to the law of God, nor indeed can be (Romans 8:5-7).

Jesus did not join Himself to the religious counterculture of His day. I am sure the people in authority were not only threatened by His ideas, but also felt He was a traitor to their cause. Jesus spent His time with the people outside the religious system. Why? He came to seek and save the lost. He came to fulfill the promise of God the Father to Abraham—that his seed would be a blessing in every nation of the earth. This sectarian, secluded Jewish culture was not that blessing.

Since Abraham shall surely become a great and mighty nation, and all the nations of the earth shall be blessed in him? (Genesis 18:18)

A CITY WITHOUT WALLS

Mankind loves to make small, comfortable, and secure worlds. God wants a big world that is not restrictive or exclusive. He wants us to be fruitful, multiply, and fill up the earth. On the other hand, we want to build little, comfortable dwellings with walls all about us to keep us separate from outside influences. But inside our religious walls created by a spirit of exclusivity and of fear, we have become a barren people. It is time for the barren to sing! It is a time of multiplication! We cannot have this great blessing until we allow our boundaries to be expanded. Father's favor can only fall on those who are willing to come outside the camp and follow Him towards their divine destiny.

"Sing, O barren, you who have not borne! Break forth into singing, and cry aloud, you who have not labored with child! For more are the children of the desolate than the children of the married woman," says the Lord. "Enlarge the place of your tent, and let them stretch out the curtains of your dwellings; do not spare; lengthen your cords, and strengthen your stakes. For you shall expand to the right and to the left,

*and your descendants will inherit the nations, and make the
desolate cities inhabited"* (Isaiah 54:1-3).

We need to expand our boundaries and tear down our walls.
This blessing of God's presence will come to a city without walls.

*Who said to him, "Run, speak to this young man, saying:
'Jerusalem shall be inhabited as towns without walls, because
of the multitude of men and livestock in it. For I,' says the
Lord, 'will be a wall of fire all around her, and I will be the glory
in her midst'"* (Zechariah 2:4-5).

PITCH YOUR OWN TENT IN THE WORLD

For the Church to attain the level of influence God wants us to
have, we must recognize we are not to develop a Christian counterculture. We are not to become a culture, but we are to impact the
cultures around us. We are to be lights in the midst of a dark world.
The light of Father's presence in our lives must shine into the
humanistic cultures around us. In a world that is crying out for a little bit of love, the Church must become a place where they will
receive acceptance rather than rejection and condemnation.

As Christians, we need to go out into the world, recognizing we
are *in* the world, but not *of* the world. We are to operate inside the
cultural institutions of our day knowing we are *in* them but certainly
not *of* them. This is why the motivation to be a witness of God in the
world is the vital principle of this move of God.

*For those who live according to the flesh set their minds on the
things of the flesh, but those who live according to the Spirit,
the things of the Spirit. For to be carnally minded is death, but
to be spiritually minded is life and peace* (Romans 8:5-6).

If our motivation is right, the Father can send us into the world
as saviors or deliverers to our generation. But we can't reach the
world if we do not first go into the world. If we are just going to sit
around, thinking they will come to us, we might be sitting for a long
time. Remember that God does not love the system, but He does
love the people in the system. He wants to have mature and responsible sons He can send into the world to seek and save the lost just

as He did when He sent His own Son into the world. Father will furnish you with His favor if you will reach out to the world as His Son reached out. Find a place to pitch your own tent in the world.

For God so loved the world that He gave His only begotten Son, that whoever believes in Him should not perish but have everlasting life. For God did not send His Son into the world to condemn the world, but that the world through Him might be saved (John 3:16-17).

Jesus was called to be the firstborn of many brethren. What He did must be duplicated in the world today. It is time for Zion to be exalted above the mountains and the saviors to come forth across the land.

But on Mount Zion there shall be deliverance, and there shall be holiness; the house of Jacob shall possess their possessions.... Then saviors shall come to Mount Zion to judge the mountains of Esau, and the kingdom shall be the Lord's (Obadiah 1:17,21).

For this great visitation of God to come forth, the people of God must break the "Christian culture" mind-set we have held on to. It is a pious pattern that has resisted the true purposes of God. But God will not exalt a system that is self-serving, rigid, legalistic, and out of touch with His Spirit. He is looking for those who are not afraid to walk by faith and who without fear will follow the Spirit.

Like Jesus Christ, in our own local church, we have had to fight the false religious mind-sets that have resisted the purposes of God in this day. We have had to confront the issue of the Christian culture that is in opposition to the plan of God for the sons of God in the earth.

We have started a Christian club at one of our community centers called 5529. The purpose of this club is to provide a viable alternative to the club culture that leads so many young people into drugs, alcohol, and promiscuous sex. Many Christians are offended that we are not propagating the Christian culture that in our day has become a multibillion dollar industry. The thinking is that we must play only "Christian" music and have "Christian" concerts. The thinking is that we first create a Christian culture, then invite the world to be a part of it.

But what makes a song Christian? The lyrics. The song must be about God or some strong Christian theme. Presumably these songs will be sung and created by other Christians. However, the secular music industry has recognized the powerful influence of "Christian" music. They have been moving in and buying out the Christian industry whenever possible. This has included purchasing book publishing companies and music companies. There goes our "Christian" music industry, sold on the block of private enterprise!

The real truth is that once money is introduced into a culture, then he who holds the cash makes the rules. This is the golden rule of humanistic economics. Money rules. The industry of "ministry" has been no exception. Note the word used is "industry." It is an *industry*, not a *ministry*. Its purpose is not to serve, but to make a profit. Because money is involved and a profit is possible, one cannot be certain as to what degree of Christianity can be applied to any segment of this industry. It isn't long before people motivated by fame and fortune begin to dominate these industries just as they do in the so-called secular side. Don't get me wrong. If a person feels they have no desire to use their gift outside of being a praise to God, I honor their sanctification. However, one must be careful not to blur the lines of sanctification in the process.

It is very clear from the Bible that whenever God is a part of something, He wants to be the center. I need lots of music to help me in the praise I offer to God. Songs of praise are a necessary part of the Christian experience. However, I have a problem when God is a part of the song but not a part of the celebration. If I am playing or listening to a love song with my wife as the inspiration, I don't want Jesus to be the sideshow. If I am dancing and having a good time at a New Year's Eve celebration, I don't intend to make

Jesus a sideshow. When He joins the scene, I believe He should be the center. Can we give Him anything less?

CHRIST AND THE CULTURE

The question then becomes, can a Christian participate in celebrations outside the celebration of Christ? The answer is a firm yes! Jesus did and He alone is the example of my life.

Till we all come to the unity of the faith and of the knowledge of the Son of God, to a perfect man, to the measure of the stature of the fullness of Christ (Ephesians 4:13).

Jesus began His ministry at a marriage supper in Cana of Galilee. When describing the celebration of the return of the prodigal son, He spoke of music and dancing. His comfort level with these things was a constant irritation to the religious establishment. Jesus understood the need to function in both the spiritual and the natural world. Jesus taught us the way to balance ourselves so we always portray ourselves as creatures of Heaven representing God to our world. Our witness shines the brightest to the world when we know how to live this testimony before people. When our light becomes visible in our everyday life, we glorify our Father who is in Heaven.

Nor do they light a lamp and put it under a basket, but on a lampstand, and it gives light to all who are in the house. Let your light so shine before men, that they may see your good works and glorify your Father in heaven (Matthew 5:15-16).

Why is the tendency to develop a Christian culture so strong? It is the result of the ascendancy of the natural man. We are walking as mere men rather than as the sons of God in the earth. There is just something within man that wants to congregate. When he congregates with others, certain habits of relationships begin to form until they become set in rock and the culturalization process has begun.

Culture is formed out of three basic human motivations. In the natural we have *affiliation needs*, the need to belong; *identification needs*, who am I in relationship to my world; and *status needs*, our need to see our value in relationship to others. These human motivations cause us to join ourselves to the world system or to create a system within our social circle to reinforce those needs. Christian culture does not serve God, but man.

How can we avoid these motivations? We must recognize we are not of this world but of the Kingdom of God. We must satisfy these desires from a heavenly perspective rather than an earthly one. The sons of God know they are not of this world but are of the Kingdom of God.

Jesus answered, "My kingdom is not of this world. If My kingdom were of this world, My servants would fight, so that I should not be delivered to the Jews; but now My kingdom is not from here." Pilate therefore said to Him, "Are You a king then?" Jesus answered, "You say rightly that I am a king. For this cause I was born, and for this cause I have come into the world, that I should bear witness to the truth. Everyone who is of the truth hears My voice" (John 18:36-37).

This goes back to our discussion in Chapter Five where Jesus was a man who knew where He came from and where He was going. Jesus also knew the present reality of His life. For Him, it was not a reality of the natural world but of the Kingdom of His Father.

When you realize you are a citizen of Heaven and not of the earth, it immediately impacts your motivation in life. Jesus was always speaking about the Kingdom of God and about motivations of the heart. These two teachings go hand in hand. If I view the world from a Kingdom perspective, it will automatically affect my motivations. When you know you are a citizen of Heaven, you realize you belong to something spiritual. Since I belong to something spiritual, my affiliation needs are not satisfied through the natural world but through the Kingdom. I must first know I belong to God. I have been redeemed. I was bought by God and I belong to Him.

For you were bought at a price; therefore glorify God in your body and in your spirit, which are God's (1 Corinthians 6:20).

You were bought at a price; do not become slaves of men
(1 Corinthians 7:23).

As a son of God, I need to realize my allegiance and purpose in life is to bring glory to God. I must see myself as being a part of the heavenly witness. This was the attitude of Jesus Christ, the firstborn Son of God, and it was also the attitude of Abraham, the Father of our faith.

These all died in faith, not having received the promises, but having seen them afar off were assured of them, embraced them and confessed that they were strangers and pilgrims on the earth. For those who say such things declare plainly that they seek a homeland (Hebrews 11:13-14).

Once we know our affiliation, then we can settle our true identity. In the natural our quest for an individual identity begins at adolescence. When we come into this world, we find our identity in our parents. When children are first born, they can't always distinguish the fact that they have their own identity. But when they get older, children begin the process of seeking their identity. Ironically, at the beginning stages, they seek their identity by finding it in some group. Often rather than assuming their own identity, they actually take on the identity of someone else. Teenagers will cry out to their parents that they want to be themselves, while their parents are watching just the opposite happen to them. In reality what they are saying is that they want the freedom to be like others who they are hanging out with.

Jesus knew who He was. Because He knew who He was, He didn't feel compelled to join the crowd. As a son of God, you will never find your identity in the crowd. You will find your true identity only when you look for it in God. This identity sets you apart for the purposes of God. You will be able to experience the Father's favor only when you learn contentment regarding how He has created you.

Set your mind on things above, not on things on the earth. For you died, and your life is hidden with Christ in God (Colossians 3:2-3).

JUST WHO ARE YOU?

Finally, we must settle the problem that has plagued mankind from the garden. It is the problem of trying to find our status by seeing our value in relationship to other people. Jesus saw Himself for who He really was. Because He saw Himself as the Son of God, He was able to respond to life and people with an air of confidence. The people around Him recognized it as an air of authority.

> *And so it was, when Jesus had ended these sayings, that the people were astonished at His teaching, for He taught them as one having authority, and not as the scribes* (Matthew 7:28-29).

When a person doesn't have anything to prove, you can hear it in their voice, and you can see it in their actions. Those who do not have to prove their worth in their words and manners will reflect a sense of confidence, and that confidence will be reflected in their countenance. It will not be the self-centered confidence that appears as arrogance or pride, but a confidence from true strength in the inner man. When the people of God see themselves as the sons of God, they will see themselves as a royal seed. What a different attitude they will have when they see their status in God. They will walk through life seeing themselves as the head and not the tail, above only and not beneath. They will be like Jesus Christ. They won't need to prove themselves to anybody, nor will they need to strive with anybody. Their status and sense of worth will not come from who they are in relationship to others, but who they are in God. They won't compare their sacrifice to their brother, as Cain did, because they will know their sacrifice is not to give them worth but to satisfy the desire of their Father in Heaven.

FINDING YOUR IDENTITY

The religious culture constantly finds itself in competition with other people or groups. This is a natural expression of a people who are trying to gain status by comparing themselves to others rather than by serving the living God. A people in this struggle will always be pointing the finger of condemnation at others rather than fulfilling their commission to show mercy and love to our world.

When Jesus heard that, He said to them, "Those who are well have no need of a physician, but those who are sick. But go and learn what this means: 'I desire mercy and not sacrifice.' For I did not come to call the righteous, but sinners, to repentance" (Matthew 9:12-13).

This was the condition of the religious establishment in the time of Jesus Christ. It is also the end result of the progression of every religious group who finds their identity and status in a religious culture. The great move of God we have seen in these last several years must prompt us to carefully examine these matters so the same thing does not come upon us. We must come to the place of revelation where we can see ourselves from the perspective of Heaven. When we see ourselves in this perspective, we will truly be the children of the Kingdom of Heaven. It will be then that we can truly fulfill our commission to be ambassadors in our world.

Now all things are of God, who has reconciled us to Himself through Jesus Christ, and has given us the ministry of reconciliation, that is, that God was in Christ reconciling the world to Himself, not imputing their trespasses to them, and has committed to us the word of reconciliation. Now then, we are ambassadors for Christ, as though God were pleading through us: we implore you on Christ's behalf, be reconciled to God (2 Corinthians 5:18-20).

Much of the Church is living in a very carnal fashion while seeing themselves as very spiritual. Their sense of belonging is satisfied in a natural way yet they call it spiritual. If your identification to the world is through your dress, you are living just as they do. You can tell a lot about a person according to what he wears. It often tells you how the person wants to be identified. Jesus wanted to be identified with Heaven. You couldn't tell by His clothes where He was from, but it wasn't long after you heard Him speak, you would know. Truly, He was not of this world. Yet, He didn't have to wear a space suit to convince you. It is time for us to recognize the need to clean up the inner man and let him shine through, rather than putting on an outward costume to impress people. Impressing God will give us greater influence in the world.

Woe to you, scribes and Pharisees, hypocrites! For you cleanse the outside of the cup and dish, but inside they are full of extortion and self-indulgence (Matthew 23:25).

Chapter Eleven

Discovering Life in Another Dimension

For if you live according to the flesh you will die; but if by the Spirit you put to death the deeds of the body, you will live (Romans 8:13).

Once we have established the need to come out of the legalist mind-set and be led by the Spirit of God, we must be very careful not to be drawn to the other extreme. We must not become a people led or motivated by the flesh. Many people will pick up on the need to come out of legalism as an excuse to live in their flesh. But you cannot live in the flesh and be pleasing to God.

And those who are Christ's have crucified the flesh with its passions and desires. If we live in the Spirit, let us also walk in the Spirit (Galatians 5:24-25).

Not only will we fail to please God when we live according to the flesh, we will also fail to reach the highest level of potential for our lives. In God's mercy He will meet us wherever we are in life. Jesus demonstrated this example in His life. Although He meets us where we are, God in His mercy also wants to lift us out of our sins and weaknesses to give us the life of an overcomer in this world.

When God in His foreknowledge created you, He made you unique with an extraordinary place in His will. The person you were created to be was both natural and spiritual. Both parts are necessary for you to fulfill your God given destiny. You must realize, however, the spiritual side of you must be the ruling part. Once you have God's Spirit, you must by the Spirit overcome the natural man so you can live according to the Spirit of life in Christ Jesus. If you live

153

according to the flesh, you will live according to the natural order, not according to the spiritual order God has ordained for your life. You will live according to the lower level, not the higher level. Don't settle for second-class living when God has called you to be a king and a priest in this world.

THE HIGH CALL OF LIFE IN CHRIST

The word "passion" in this verse refers to the emotional influences we have in our life. It specifically refers to emotions resulting from hardships we have gone through in life. The word "desire" speaks of any lust or motivating influence from our heart, or simply put, our bodily desires. All these things can hinder us from reaching our calling in life. We must be mindful that our calling in God is a calling to something higher than who we are right now, something beyond our human capacity. God's call to you is an upward call.

> *Brethren, I do not count myself to have apprehended; but one thing I do, forgetting those things which are behind and reaching forward to those things which are ahead, I press toward the goal for the prize of the upward call of God in Christ Jesus* (Philippians 3:13-14).

We must recognize it is also God's mercy not to let us live below His desire for us. We are living in a day when people tend to perceive love only as a willingness to accept us for who we are. The cry of the day is "love me for who I am!" We want people to accept us without expectations and desires from us. This attitude may make you comfortable at first, but in the end it will leave you miserable. You see, God does love you for who you are. The trouble is He knows who you are better than you know yourself. He knows your capabilities and also your present heart's desire. And if you will follow Him and allow His Word to work in you, you will truly find your heart's desire.

> *Delight yourself also in the Lord, and He shall give you the desires of your heart* (Psalm 37:4).

As God's Spirit directs us towards becoming a full heir son, it will lead us into a place beyond our natural capabilities. Sometimes we will think that the process is more than we can handle. When we find ourselves in situations that seem to stretch us beyond ourselves, then our human desire will be to turn back or get relief. We need to understand that God is seeking to take us to a place where we are forced to draw on His strength and become perfected in Him. Paul, the apostle, had this struggle. He had a weakness in his flesh that he didn't like. Although there has been much debate on what the weakness was, the real issue was his response to that weakness. As many of us do, he cried out to God for deliverance. But God's answer was not what Paul wanted to hear.

> *Concerning this thing I pleaded with the Lord three times that it might depart from me. And He said to me, "My grace is sufficient for you, for My strength is made perfect in weakness." Therefore most gladly I will rather boast in my infirmities, that the power of Christ may rest upon me* (2 Corinthians 12:8-9).

LIFE IN ANOTHER DIMENSION

God wanted Paul to live a life beyond his own natural abilities. Paul was accustomed to being able to persevere and handle any situation. His natural personality and abilities were very strong. Now he was being taken to the very end of himself. Once you reach that place, then God can take you into another dimension where you will experience the power of His life. You see, God did not call you to live apart from Him. He called you and created you as a person who would be complete only in Him.

> *And you are complete in Him, who is the head of all principality and power* (Colossians 2:10).

When God said His grace would be sufficient for Paul, many people assume this to mean God was encouraging Paul to be content with life as it was. God's grace is not equal to God telling us to be content with where we are. God's grace is God's ability working in our weakness to demonstrate the power of God. God's strength then becomes perfected in our weakness. We become strong not through our own ability, but through the power of God. As we begin to live this life from another dimension, we begin to see that there is a capacity for life beyond anything we could ever generate in ourselves.

To get to this place of strength, we must get beyond ourselves into the power of God. We have limited God and ourselves by trying to bring God down to our world rather than letting God bring us up to His. It is time for the Church to step beyond the ordinary into the extraordinary—the supernatural. God longs to reveal His glory through His sons, but this glory can shine only from that other dimension. It cannot be revealed unless we are willing to suffer in the flesh by being willing to move beyond our comfort zone into God's strength zone. God is calling you out of your comfort zone! God wants to bring you to the dimension of faith where you live beyond yourself and live by the power of God. If you will be drawn into this discomfort, then the glory of God can be revealed through you.

And if children, then heirs—heirs of God and joint heirs with Christ, if indeed we suffer with Him, that we may also be glorified together. For I consider that the sufferings of this present time are not worthy to be compared with the glory which shall be revealed in us (Romans 8:17-18).

BEYOND THE COMFORT ZONE INTO THE STRENGTH ZONE

Jesus Himself was faced with this challenge in the garden of Gethsemane. The time had come and Jesus knew that Father was asking Him to go to the cross, to fulfill His eternal destiny. The man, Christ Jesus, knew the pain and agony of the commitment that would take Him beyond His human comfort zone. He would face emotional and physical pain beyond the normal limits of life. Like us, He was counting the cost. He wanted to do the will of His Father, but would He be able to stand against the horrific physical abuse and emotional pain that He was about to step into?

Jesus had descended into the world of man exchanging His robe of glory for the rags of human flesh. He was not immune to any human experience. He had experienced every temptation common to all men. This had been a necessary part of the walk. Yet, like us, He would be able to draw on the power of the Spirit for the journey and ultimately receive the greatest power of all. In the garden He found the favor of Father and was energized by His strength so that He could face the ultimate test. He would receive the power of resurrection from the dead. His response to God must have found favor with His Father as He opened the door to the Father's will.

He went a little farther and fell on His face, and prayed, saying, "O My Father, if it is possible, let this cup pass from Me; nevertheless, not as I will, but as You will" (Matthew 26:39).

THE ULTIMATE PAIN—REJECTION BY THOSE YOU LOVE

After He consented to the Father's will, Jesus faced unbearable suffering. Typically, when we think of the cross, we think of the great physical pain Jesus suffered. This was certainly a great challenge. The greatest challenge, however, was the emotional stress He had to face. I can say this from personal experience and also from many years of dealing with the people of God. Jesus had to experience the greatest of emotional pains—the pain of rejection. We usually think of death as the worst pain of all. The loss of a loved one is a very trying experience, yet it can be much worse to suffer the loss of someone because they have rejected us.

When Jesus went to the cross, He went alone. Even as He hung there on the cross, most of His followers had abandoned Him. Where were the disciples? They said they would go with Him anywhere. The most chilling sense of rejection was portrayed in the words Jesus spoke from the cross:

Now when the sixth hour had come, there was darkness over the whole land until the ninth hour. And at the ninth hour Jesus cried out with a loud voice, saying, "Eloi, Eloi, lama sabachthani?" which is translated, "My God, My God, why have You forsaken Me?" (Mark 15:33-34)

There was indeed darkness on the whole land, but the darkness in Jesus' soul was greater than any darkness He had ever experienced. He groaned deeply as the pangs of Father's seeming rejection swept over Him. He hung on the cross—alone. I wonder if the Scripture of Isaiah was on His mind?

Yet it pleased the Lord to bruise Him; He has put Him to grief.
When You make His soul an offering for sin, He shall see His
seed, He shall prolong His days, and the pleasure of the Lord
shall prosper in His hand (Isaiah 53:10).

DEATH LEADS TO RESURRECTION POWER

It was His Father's pleasure to bruise Him! Why? It was
because the Father saw His seed. He saw you and me, His children,
serving Him in the generations to come. Jesus had to reconcile His
pain with the Father's desire. He had to let His suffering run its
course to allow the purpose of the Father to come to pass. Yet, in so
doing He also opened the door to the power of the resurrection. It
was this holiness to the Lord that would be the source of the power
of His resurrection. The path that He was willing to take, the path of
consecration to the will of the Father, opened a doorway that would
release Heaven's power.

And declared to be the Son of God with power according to
the Spirit of holiness, by the resurrection from the dead
(Romans 1:4).

Today we, the sons of God, must understand that our Father in
Heaven will allow us to suffer if it contributes to His purpose. The
Word declares all things work together for the good to those who
love God and are called according to His purpose. Of course, we
have to define what is good. Sometimes, the path of pain becomes a
good thing because it will lead us into new dimensions of spiritual
reality—places that we could not have reached in any other way. In
the end, the crisis we face for the Father will lend itself to good
things. We, as the mature sons of God, must recognize that suffering
is a part of our journey, but that it is not senseless suffering. Our
suffering can be the source of accomplishing the Father's purposes
in this world. The only way to resurrection is through a death.

We are living in the day when God will reveal the ultimate
dynamics of His power through His people. This is the day for resurrection power, and it will be revealed through the sons of God. The
sons who give themselves to the purpose of the Father without limi-
tations will be the sons who reveal God's power to their generation.

Resurrection power is the power beyond our human ability. It is beyond us. And we cannot experience this power unless we get beyond ourselves. We must die to get resurrection power.

For some, the call beyond yourself is letting go of some emotional hold on your life; for some, it is a physical hold. God wants you to know if you will step beyond yourself, He will meet you at the point of your surrender with the power of resurrection life. Something inside of you is calling you to live beyond yourself—to step over into that dimension of life with God. Something is beckoning you to the higher place. That call is the eternal purpose of God—the destiny that God has had for you even before you were born. Don't run from your purpose because you don't think you can do it. The truth is that you can't do it. Remember it is "Christ in you" that will be your hope and strength.

> *The mystery which has been hidden from ages and from generations, but now has been revealed to His saints. To them God willed to make known what are the riches of the glory of this mystery among the Gentiles: which is Christ in you, the hope of glory* (Colossians 1:26-27).

THE CHOICES MADE IN THE SECRET PLACE

In the summer of 1993, I was feeling a special call from God and was sensing that He wanted a greater commitment from me on a personal level, so I made a covenant with God of personal holiness. Remember that the Father's reward in the public places will come from what He sees in the secret place. The decisions that you make in the private places will lead to success in the open places.

> *But when you do a charitable deed, do not let your left hand know what your right hand is doing, that your charitable deed may be in secret; and your Father who sees in secret will Himself reward you openly* (Matthew 6:3-4).

As a sign of my covenant, I chose to wear a gold cross around my neck. It was not a cross to be seen as jewelry, but one held secretly next to my heart. When I went to purchase the cross, it was given to me as a present instead. To me this was a sign of

God's grace. Our covenant faithfulness is only possible with His grace. I had a good spiritual experience that day and felt very comfortable that I would be walking into a time of greater blessing from the Father.

But as I mentioned earlier, during the next summer of 1994, I went through the greatest trial of my life. I started having seizures on a daily basis. This trial lasted nine months before God healed me. In the middle of the trial, I was having an especially very difficult time. I don't know if it was the medication or the affliction. Sometimes the cure is worse than the disease. All my life I had a special sense of the presence of God, and it was this presence that sustained me through the difficulties of life. But now I was going through a time when I did not feel God's presence. It was difficult enough just suffering the physical infirmity, yet now I had to face a great emotional time without the sense of God's presence. Whether the cause was the medication or the affliction, the sense of abandonment and not feeling God's presence was my greatest hardship during this trial of my faith.

WHERE ARE YOU, GOD?

One day when I was in prayer, I cried out in anguish to the Lord. I could stand the affliction, but how could He not comfort me in this time of great stress? I felt alone, deserted by the God I had given my whole life for. Earlier in my life I had experienced a great physical ordeal with my muscles. I had been diagnosed with muscular dystrophy. It was a time of great physical pain and emotional distress as well. But I can say God's presence seemed very real through the whole process. I had been healed of that affliction so I knew God's power could heal. Yet, I had never been left with the feeling of being alone, without God's presence close by. I became angry with God and I let Him know it!

In that moment of time, the Scripture was quickened to me, regarding Jesus asking the Father how He could have forsaken Him. At that moment I remembered my cross and my covenant of consecration. I had told the Father my life belonged to Him. I wanted to do what He asked of me. I understood "in part" the agony of the

160

only begotten Son. For the first time in my life, I had a glimpse of the cross.

Now the call of a true disciple was no small matter.

Then He said to them all, "If anyone desires to come after Me, let him deny himself, and take up his cross daily, and follow Me. For whoever desires to save his life will lose it, but whoever loses his life for My sake will save it" (Luke 9:23-24).

I had never realized it before, but in my walk with God I had basically said, "God, I will do whatever You want me to do. I will do it as long as You make me feel good when I am doing it." I had the attitude of the drug addict who can get through life only with the right feeling. I didn't realize it, but my emotions had become an obstacle to obedience. In 40 years of serving God, I had been faithful and obedient. Now I would have to win this battle with a strength that went beyond my natural strength and beyond my emotions.

There is a growing body of evidence that our brain contains a certain part that gives us a sense of religious consciousness. This part causes us to be aware and experience religious feelings. This is God's gift. It is the candle of the Lord. In my reading, I also found it is this particular part that is suppressed by seizure medication. Whether my sense of abandonment was physical or spiritual, it was very real. All the elements of my ordeal were necessary to take me beyond my emotional response to God. God wanted to have my heart and my will. He wanted me to find my purpose totally in Him. It was only from this place that I could be a true son of God. Here, in this new place, the great power of God could be released in my life.

In the past I had always been obedient, and my favorite Scripture was the one found in Hebrews 1:9:

You have loved righteousness and hated lawlessness; therefore God, Your God, has anointed You with the oil of gladness more than Your companions (Hebrews 1:9).

I have always enjoyed doing what God wanted me to do. Obedience was not difficult; it was a delight. Yet, at this time of crisis, I felt God had forsaken me. How could He take this great joy from me? In my mind, I felt God was unjust, and during the length of the trial, I began to spew out my anger towards Him. God always assured me though, that He would reward my righteousness. The inner assurance of the Word always came, but without the normal feeling to which I was accustomed. God was teaching me about walking in the Spirit beyond feelings. He was breaking a barrier to true sonship. The barriers we have from our own emotional dispositions can be contrary to the truth of God. Feelings are so subjective; they come and go. We all are easily affected by the smallest shift in our environment. A true son must learn to not be shaken by what is happening around him. And the only way to learn these things is to walk through them.

It is funny as I reflect now upon some of my attitudes that I thought were godly, only to realize they were just my emotional temperament at the time. Once God broke the stronghold of my natural emotional disposition, I could truly be ready to be led by the Spirit and follow His will and His desire. I want to share two of my personal characteristics, formed from my emotional disposition, which could have been easily confused with godliness.

One revelation came when I realized that I thought I was nicer than God was. In my mind, since God was love, God would certainly always be nice. When the Word spoke of the goodness of God, I had always related it to "niceness." I didn't like mean and ornery people. I always liked being around people with a desire to treat others "nice." The word *nice* means to be pleasing and agreeable. I was learning the hard way God isn't always nice. God doesn't always do everything He can to please me, and He certainly doesn't always agree with me. You see, we are created for His pleasure and to demonstrate His Word to our world. Sometimes we must break our emotional bonds to really be the person He wants us to be. Too many people try to create God in *their* image rather than let Him create them in *His* image.

Our society today demands certain things out of people. If you love me, they say, then you will treat me like I want to be treated. God says, "If you love Me, you will do what I ask of you."

If you ask anything in My name, I will do it. If you love Me, keep My commandments (John 14:14-15).

WHOSE WORLD ARE YOU LIVING IN?

Too many people today want the power of God demonstrated in their life but do not want to accept the responsibility of true sonship. We want to continue to look at the world from our philosophy of living. We take polls from those around us and let those results determine how we will live our life. We try to squeeze God into our little world rather than letting ourselves die to go into His world, but God is too big for our world. During my physical ordeal, God was using this circumstance for my enlargement. He wanted to bring me into His world, that is, His Kingdom, so He could reveal His glory in me.

IS YOUR WORLD TOO SMALL?

In yet another way my emotional condition limited me—it made my world too small. I had a false sense of holiness that made it difficult for me to fully function in my world. Since I served the Lord from childhood, I had built up many holiness standards that were more fleshly piety than the true holiness of God. When I first started preaching the Word, I experienced a real dilemma. One day while preparing to preach, I was reading the scriptures when I came upon the word "ass." This will sound silly to many, but I had never said the word "ass" out loud. I was a good Christian boy and did not cuss. And "ass" was a cuss word to me. I was too embarrassed to say the word so I just substituted the word "donkey." If that wasn't bad enough, I came across the word "pisseth." Was I ever glad when the New King James Version came out so I could switch Bibles and quit cussing! Just think I was so holy, I was holier than the Holy Bible! This might be silly, but believe me there is a lot of "silliness" in the Body of Christ.

I was preparing to preach a message from Zechariah 9:9, and God was speaking to me about the fact that He was looking for a "donkey" to ride upon. In my research, I realized that Israel had a wide variety of asses and not all were domesticated. The word "donkey" cannot be used to describe all categories of asses. The word "donkey" implies a hybrid mixture, not necessarily a pure ass. I realized God didn't want to use a half-ass for His purposes. For God, sometimes only a full "ass" will do. I guess you're getting the real point here.

If I had wanted to convey the full meaning of the Scripture, I wouldn't have wanted to use the word "donkey," but the word "ass." This caused a conflict within me at first, but then it released me to be free of my personal embarrassment or consciousness to declare the Word of God. It was time for me to quit being holier than the Bible. God used that message to thoroughly purge my religious nature. The sense of holiness and the difficulty of using these words were signals to me of how my emotions and feelings could hinder me from doing what God wanted me to do. This could isolate me from the people God wanted me to help. This is why we must get beyond emotional dispositions and spiritual pride that can seem so right and yet actually be opposed to the plan of God. Vain religion and self-righteous justification can destroy the move of God in your life.

Before the Lord worked these principles in my life, I could have easily been one of the scribes and the Pharisees who resisted the Lord Jesus Himself when He walked on the earth. I certainly could have criticized His worldly ways and His permissive attitudes. I wouldn't have liked His friends or been as patient with sinners as He was. I, like the Pharisees, could have been more concerned about punishment than mercy. I could have been like His disciples when they asked Jesus if He wanted them to call down fire from Heaven on the Samaritans. I too would have received the rebuke He gave His disciples who thought they were right with Jesus but were actually of a whole different spirit.

And when His disciples James and John saw this, they said, "Lord, do You want us to command fire to come down from heaven and consume them, just as Elijah did?" But He turned and rebuked them, and said, "You do not know what manner of spirit you are of. For the Son of Man did not come to destroy men's lives but to save them." And they went to another village (Luke 9:54-56).

You see, living by the Spirit is not as easy as we suppose. Yet, God in this day is bringing a people to the other side of the veil. It is time to go into the inner court of God's presence. It is time to behold the mercy seat and become the true ministers of righteousness. Like Jesus, the firstborn Son, we must allow the rending of the veil of our flesh. As we step over into that dimension, the power of God will be released in new ways through our lives.

Therefore, brethren, having boldness to enter the Holiest by the blood of Jesus, by a new and living way which He consecrated for us, through the veil, that is, His flesh (Hebrews 10:19-20).

Chapter Twelve

The Power of a Renewed Mind

For to be carnally minded is death, but to be spiritually minded is life and peace. Because the carnal mind is enmity against God; for it is not subject to the law of God, nor indeed can be (Romans 8:6-7).

To be a true son of God in the earth, we need to have a spiritual mind—the mind of Christ. Many Christians, especially charismatic and Pentecostal Christians, think of the mind as the enemy of God. The mind is not the enemy but a key element of what God will use to bring us to the place of walking in His perfect will. The point is that we must understand there is a difference between the carnal mind and the spiritual mind. Because of the fall, man's mind was darkened and became alienated from God. When we come to Christ, our minds must go under a process of renewal. Once we understand this, we can be a people with the right mind. Unfortunately, many Christians in the past have decided that since the mind hinders the purpose of God, we must by-pass the mind or get rid of our intellect. This is not the case. Christians should possess the greatest minds of the time and truly set the pace of creative genius!

In the beginning of time, God created His first son, Adam. He was a unique creation of God. Adam was a creature created from both the earth and Heaven. The reason scientists suppose we are of the same species as the animal kingdom is because they see the similarities of our fleshly makeup. They see an amazing closeness in our DNA to the animals, especially the apes. One could easily be deceived on this matter without the consultation of the Word. However, in the Word of God, we find a great difference.

When we were formed from the dust of the earth, God breathed in us the breath of life. This was the breath of Heaven, a breath of the divine. We would take on the image of the heavenly Father by being spiritual beings, yet living in bodies of flesh. There is no scientific instrument capable of analyzing our spiritual DNA.

THE SPIRITUAL DNA OF MAN

And the Lord God formed man of the dust of the ground, and breathed into his nostrils the breath of life; and man became a living being (Genesis 2:7).

Many animals breathe, but God gave to us *His* breath, the "breath of life." This "breath of life" is what we call the human spirit. The human spirit gives us a consciousness of God. It is our link to the dimension where God lives. By the spirit we can communicate and have fellowship with the Father.

The spirit of a man is the lamp of the Lord, searching all the inner depths of his heart (Proverbs 20:27).

We are not only conscious of God, but we have self-conscious thought as well. We have the capacity to think and reason and analyze. We are created with a God-given ability to reflect upon our relationships, our world, and ourselves. This makes us uniquely suited to become true sons of God. Only man has the ability to have a relationship with God and only man is created in a way to operate as agents of dominion on the earth. What a wonderful work "the sons of God" have been given!

The Scriptures also inform us that this merging of the natural and divine breath of God would produce a creature of understanding. Man would be able to think and reason about those responses that he would make to the environment around him.

But there is a spirit in man, and the breath of the Almighty gives him understanding (Job 32:8).

The word "understanding" in the Scriptures implies the ability to separate things. True wisdom is the ability to make distinctions between what is emotional, physical, spiritual, and also reasonable.

Adam could walk in harmony with his Father, his environment, and with himself.

WE NEED PEOPLE

God sealed man's destiny by creating woman, authenticating the human need for companionship and community. It is important to note when Adam was alone, it was God who took note of the problem and corrected it. It was not Adam's observation. God did not create His sons to be alone nor did He create us just for Himself. He created us in a way that we would need others to complete our life. It is amazing how many people think that to be spiritual, you must be separate. We are afraid that if we come in contact with other mortal beings, we might become infected somehow. This is not true. A spiritual person longs to be with other people and enjoys caring for other people!

When God created His sons, He created us for a purpose. The purpose is fellowship and partnership with God. One without the other does not fulfill the plan of God. Many people love fellowship with God but won't accept their place as partners with God. We are created for the Father's purpose. On the other hand, many people want to do something for God without fellowship and communion. Jesus established this principle with the disciples. He first called them to be with Him, but there would come a time that He would send them out to the people.

Then He appointed twelve, that they might be with Him and that He might send them out to preach (Mark 3:14).

PARTNERS WITH THE FATHER

The first Adam was placed in the Garden of Eden. Through him mankind was given a mandate of dominion. As God gave to Adam, so God gives to each of us a special stewardship, a part of the world He has entrusted to our care and responsibility. Like the first son, Adam, we must recognize our need for responsible stewardship by guarding and developing what the Father has put into our hands. True spiritual sons have discovered the territory that Father has entrusted into their hands and have dedicated themselves to the fulfillment of that task.

Then the Lord God took the man and put him in the garden of Eden to tend and keep it (Genesis 2:15).

The key to partnership with God is always recognizing we are the junior partners.

God said to Adam:

And the Lord God commanded the man, saying, "Of every tree of the garden you may freely eat; but of the tree of the knowledge of good and evil you shall not eat, for in the day that you eat of it you shall surely die" (Genesis 2:16-17).

There was plenty of work to keep Adam occupied. He was given vast freedom and enormous responsibility in Father's world. Yet, there was also a certain location to which he was denied access. The Father gave the warning for Adam's good. God knew when He told Adam that in the day he ate of the fruit of the tree of knowledge of good and evil, he would die. We must understand this was not just a punishment. It would be the consequences of a wrong choice. The Word declares this as the principle of sowing and reaping. God was forced to take Adam out of the garden to protect the creation and the purpose He had for mankind. If Adam had stayed in the garden, he could have lived forever in his sinful state and there would have been no end to the dominion of sin.

Then the Lord God said, "Behold, the man has become like one of Us, to know good and evil. And now, lest he put out his hand and take also of the tree of life, and eat, and live forever"—therefore the Lord God sent him out of the garden of Eden to till the ground from which he was taken (Genesis 3:22-23).

WHO'S THE BOSS?

Although God has a great plan for mankind, there are still some things God withholds for Himself. If we are willing to give God His part, He has much He wants to give us in return. We must

170

never forget that He is God and we are humans. This is what the principle of tithing is all about. If we give God our firstfruits, we sanctify the whole lump. We give God ten percent as an act of worship, and He lets us keep the ninety percent. That is a pretty good deal when you understand it all actually belongs to God. It is time for the people of God to open their eyes to the awesomeness of what God wants to do for them and through them.

Instead, we fight with God's plans trying to direct God and tell Him what to do for us. We think we have greater wisdom than He does. If God would just listen to us, "how much better the world would be" is our attitude! We want to create a god from the works of our hands—something we can control. But the God of the universe wants to make us a partner in His eternal plan. The prophet, Isaiah, declared the foolishness of this attitude:

Who has directed the Spirit of the Lord, or as His counselor has taught Him? With whom did He take counsel, and who instructed Him, and taught Him in the path of justice? Who taught Him knowledge, and showed Him the way of understanding? (Isaiah 40:13-14)

Since God won't listen to us, we create a god we can fashion to our desire. The end result is a powerless and unsatisfactory life outside the will and the purpose of God. This is what happened to Adam, and this is what happens to many of the children of God. We don't trust that God has a plan for our life that includes a wonderful destiny for our life.

However, just the opposite is true.

Trust in the Lord, and do good; dwell in the land, and feed on His faithfulness. Delight yourself also in the Lord, and He shall give you the desires of your heart. Commit your way to the Lord, trust also in Him, and He shall bring it to pass (Psalm 37:3-5).

A HIGHWAY CALLED TRUST

The path of life will always begin when man begins to trust God. We may not understand or see the end, but when you trust in God, wherever the road takes you will be okay.

We need to let God be our delight. We need to find true satisfaction in Him. This will keep us in a position of patient endurance. If your focus is on your circumstances, they will bring you down. True spiritual sons have learned to rise above their circumstances and focus on Father who is at work in His dimension. Our natural eyes are too shortsighted and cannot see the long view where God is working out His purposes in our lives. As we allow ourselves to be conformed to His way, we can be sure God will bring to pass the things we couldn't do for ourselves. It begins with trust and will be consummated in trust.

Adam and Eve did not trust God, so they decided to take matters into their own hands. The end result was a horrible isolation from God and the beginning of a road that would lead them far from Father's domain. What road will you choose? The road of human thinking is a road to bondage. The road back home is the road of trust. You have to trust the road map created by the Spirit to bring you back to your destiny in God. Any other pathway will lead you to a prison of dreadful bondage.

While they promise them liberty, they themselves are slaves of corruption; for by whom a person is overcome, by him also he is brought into bondage (2 Peter 2:19).

This prison of sin results in a mind alienated from God. It degenerates into a mind that operates in the darkness of our own understanding, outside the will and the purpose of God. It is a mind without true perception of spiritual realities.

This I say, therefore, and testify in the Lord, that you should no longer walk as the rest of the Gentiles walk, in the futility of their mind, having their understanding darkened, being alienated from the life of God, because of the ignorance that is in them, because of the blindness of their heart; who, being past feeling, have given themselves over to lewdness, to work all uncleanness with greediness (Ephesians 4:17-19).

A MIND WITHOUT GOD

A mind without God will lead to all kinds of evil. One only has to look at history to see the depravity of the human mind and all the evil that can result. Knowledge without God will lead to death and destruction. The last century is a good example of this. The 1900s began with the industrial revolution, and the world witnessed greater educational and technological advances than history had ever known. Although we certainly saw technological advancement, we also saw wars that killed multiplied millions. Our technology that gave us an easier life has also threatened our existence with the ongoing creation of all kinds of weapons of mass destruction. The threat of ultimate destruction through nuclear war has hung over the last half of the century as a dark cloud of disaster. We saw the horrors of genocide as people destroyed one another in hate—Iraq, Somalia, Nigeria, Yugoslavia, and others. Our knowledge has not made us so sophisticated that we are able to overcome the basest of human emotions—hate and prejudice.

Man, without the knowledge of God, will not produce life, but in the end will destroy life.

And even as they did not like to retain God in their knowledge, God gave them over to a debased mind, to do those things which are not fitting; being filled with all unrighteousness, sexual immorality, wickedness, covetousness, maliciousness; full of envy, murder, strife, deceit, evil-mindedness; they are whisperers (Romans 1:28-29).

THIS LITTLE LIGHT OF MINE

The world needs God; the Father needs His sons. In the midst of darkness, God the Father is looking to radiate His light into the world of man through His people. Jesus came as the light. We are called to be children of the light. A cosmic darkness has filled our world producing confusion, fear, acts of terror, deceit, and total alienation. The hope for this world is not to be found in a political solution. It can only be found in a community of people who have stepped into the light of Father's glory and are now reflecting that light back into their world.

While you have the light, believe in the light, that you may become sons of light (John 12:36).

For you were once darkness, but now you are light in the Lord. Walk as children of light (for the fruit of the Spirit is in all goodness, righteousness, and truth), finding out what is acceptable to the Lord (Ephesians 5:8-10).

It is time for the sons of God to arise as the light of the world. It is time for the Church to be all that the Father has called it to be and let the light shine from our works for God.

You are the light of the world. A city that is set on a hill cannot be hidden. Nor do they light a lamp and put it under a basket, but on a lampstand, and it gives light to all who are in the house. Let your light so shine before men, that they may see your good works and glorify your Father in heaven (Matthew 5:14-16).

God, our Father, has not called us to be watchers of the darkness. He has not called us to fear the darkness nor sit around moaning about the darkness. God has called us to be a light in the midst of the darkness. He has called us to be a people who understand that darkness is the absence of light. Darkness has no source in itself. It is created by a deficit of light. In the day when darkness is upon the land and gross darkness the people, God will do a great work through His people who believe Him at His word. When God's people are connected again to the Source of all light, then His glory will again return to the earth regions of man.

Arise, shine; for your light has come! And the glory of the Lord is risen upon you. For behold, the darkness shall cover the earth, and deep darkness the people; but the Lord will arise over you, and His glory will be seen upon you (Isaiah 60:1-2).

The work of God's light, of course, must begin in us. The source of darkness is the depraved mind without God. The source of light into the world will shine from a restored mind radiating through the life of the sons of God. We need to have the mind God wants us to have. When we come to the Lord, we must recognize God wants to restore all we have lost through the sin of Adam. Just as through Adam's sin all men die, through the life of Jesus Christ, the last Adam, we can all live. Life is a journey, and the journey will take us down the road of "process" where we are gradually being restored back to our original condition. We cannot go forward until we go back and recapture all that was lost by the first Adam.

For since by man came death, by Man also came the resurrection of the dead. For as in Adam all die, even so in Christ all shall be made alive (1 Corinthians 15:21-22).

We must understand Jesus Christ did not come just to make us alive, but He also came to restore all that Adam lost by the big deception in the garden.

For if when we were enemies we were reconciled to God through the death of His Son, much more, having been reconciled, we shall be saved by His life (Romans 5:10).

THE PROCESS LEADS TO A PROMISE OF LIFE

Many Christians think once they have been reconciled to God, that is the end of the salvation experience. Salvation to many people is a fire insurance policy protecting them from hell. We need to understand God's salvation is much more than that. Jesus came into the world not just to make us alive, but also to give us the abundant life by giving back what the enemy has stolen. Once we have been restored, then the process will bring us to the place of promise where we are empowered to regain our place that was stolen by the enemy.

The thief does not come except to steal, and to kill, and to destroy. I have come that they may have life, and that they may have it more abundantly (John 10:10).

As is noted in Ephesians 4, this process begins by being reconciled back to the life of God. Once we have this life, then we need to allow the transformation of our life to include all the Father desires for us. This process can only find its fullness when we are reconciled to God and have our minds transformed to the mind God wants us to have.

I beseech you therefore, brethren, by the mercies of God, that you present your bodies a living sacrifice, holy, acceptable to

*God, which is your reasonable service. And do not be con-
formed to this world, but be transformed by the renewing of
your mind, that you may prove what is that good and acceptable and perfect will of God* (Romans 12:1-2).

God intended us to be people of understanding with a clear
and good mind. This process of restoring the mind does not begin
with the pursuit of knowledge. It is not *information* that we need,
but *inspiration*. We need light to flood into our minds, and that light
will heal and cleanse all the dark places in our thinking and reasoning. It begins by us opening ourselves to the source of all true
knowledge, the Spirit of God. Our renovation must begin in the
spirit of our mind.

*That you put off, concerning your former conduct, the old man
which grows corrupt according to the deceitful lusts, and be
renewed in the spirit of your mind, and that you put on the new
man which was created according to God, in true righteousness
and holiness* (Ephesians 4:22-24).

Note that the new man comes from the renewed mind. We
often try to work on being the new man without a new mind. This
is an important principle. Man tries to clean up the outside first.
But God starts from the inside and then works to the exterior. We
often try to shine the light of God through works of flesh without
having a renewed spirit, and the end result will always be flesh
works and vain religion. Vain religion, as we see in our world today,
is just as dangerous as the mind without God. We must begin with
His Spirit. And when we receive the Spirit of God, we experience
something beyond our understanding. Paul indicates that when we
speak by the Spirit, it is our spirit speaking and not our mind.

WALKING BY THE SPIRIT

*For if I pray in a tongue, my spirit prays, but my understanding
is unfruitful* (1 Corinthians 14:14).

Many Christians struggle with this concept. Why would I want
to pray when I don't know what I am saying? This mind-set has the
obvious reason within itself. The human mind wants to control its

surroundings and to control God. The Word instructs us to begin the restoration by giving up our understanding and control, and letting God do a work in us. Let your spirit come alive. Walk into a dimension beyond yourself. Many people struggle after receiving the Holy Spirit over the issue of how walking by the Spirit works. This is an indication we are in a struggle learning to walk beyond our understanding. Give up and let God do something for you beyond your understanding. The goal of the Pentecostal experience is not to get you to speak in tongues but to teach you to walk in the Spirit. Because most of us are guided by our minds and we are people of the flesh, part of our spiritual transformation into sons should be to learn how to live in the dimension of the Spirit.

I first received the Holy Spirit in a Pentecostal church. The goal, even in our services, was the practice of reaching beyond ourselves to find God. In the early days of the movement, people didn't even think someone should prepare a sermon. We should just flow with the Spirit and speak whatever came to us. We thought that any order in worship or sermon preparation was simply a lack of faith. Unfortunately, many have never gone beyond this concept. Although we need to begin our experience operating from the Spirit and not the mind, it should not be our goal. Our goal is a renewed mind. With a renewed mind, we are ready for the Spirit to take us to the next level in Him.

After World War II, there was a fresh move of God. The latter rain and healing movements were the foundation for the birth of the charismatic movement. This brought a whole new dimension to the Pentecostal experience. The people of God began to see the fresh patterns of God's activity through His Word. We learned that you don't just wait for the Spirit to move upon you; you can see and follow the patterns of the Word to give the Spirit the proper outlet. We don't just "dance in the Spirit"; we dance before the Lord. We don't just wait for the moving of the Spirit; we initiate it through worship and praise. We don't just tarry for the Spirit; we lay hands on people and impart the Holy Spirit. The Church could relate now to the Holy Spirit with the knowledge of the Word. Pentecostals resisted this practice, but those who flowed with new understanding began to experience a great blessing from the promises of God. If all we do is continue to "wait," then we will never get the work done. There is a place for "waiting" but Father has given us a new mind, and by the power of His Spirit we can know what we should be doing during these critical times in which we are living.

The teaching movement that came in the '70s also brought a release of much power to the Church. We are not to be ignorant of God's Word or, for that matter, any knowledge available to us. Once we have been enlightened, we need to come out of ignorance so we can have the knowledge of the Lord.

> *My people are destroyed for lack of knowledge. Because you have rejected knowledge, I also will reject you from being priest for Me; because you have forgotten the law of your God, I also will forget your children* (Hosea 4:6).

THE TRUE SOURCE OF ALL KNOWLEDGE

For the human mind to operate in its highest levels, we must understand the importance of the proper heart motivations and emotional influences that impact our thinking, often without us even knowing it. Contemporary society is only now beginning to see the importance of "emotional intelligence." Logical processing of information is good when calculating math equations, but certainly is not sufficient when dealing with the issues of life. John Forbes Nash, a Nobel Peace Prize winner, said that he had always believed in numbers, but it is only in the *mysterious equations of love* that any logic can be found!

Modern society has elevated knowledge and rationalism to a place where it provides the only solution to true understanding in life. This is the basis of modern psychology, medicine, philosophy, and political thought. Multitudes of people now have a greater understanding of the nature of their problems but are still unable to resolve them. The medical field is now finding our emotions are a big part of a person's physical well-being, either negatively or positively. Many are even researching the power of prayer as they are clearly seeing the impact of one's spiritual life on their health. In the circles of government, politicians are beginning to see political and economic systems alone will not cure what ails a society. We are at the dawn of a new age of understanding, and I believe the Church has the opportunity to stand at the cutting edge of the incoming revolution.

If we want to walk with the wisdom and understanding God intended from the beginning, we must see how important it is to include our heart in the equation.

So that you incline your ear to wisdom, and apply your heart to understanding (Proverbs 2:2).

We must realize the root of darkness lies within our desire to express our own heart rather than to have the heart of God.

A fool has no delight in understanding, but in expressing his own heart (Proverbs 18:2).

In humility, we must understand the only way we can have a heart change is to give ourselves over to the work of God and let Him give us a new heart.

The heart is deceitful above all things, and desperately wicked; who can know it? I, the Lord, search the heart, I test the mind, even to give every man according to his ways, according to the fruit of his doings (Jeremiah 17:9-10).

We must open our heart to God and ask Him to lead us along the path to a new heart.

Search me, O God, and know my heart; try me, and know my anxieties; and see if there is any wicked way in me, and lead me in the way everlasting (Psalm 139:23-24).

God promises in His covenant with us to give us a new heart and a new spirit.

I will give you a new heart and put a new spirit within you; I will take the heart of stone out of your flesh and give you a heart of flesh. I will put My Spirit within you and cause you to walk in My statutes, and you will keep My judgments and do them (Ezekiel 36:26-27).

Mankind was made in the image and likeness of God. When considering the concepts of body, soul, and spirit, we must see them like the Trinity of God Himself, as distinctions but not separations. With this in mind, we can simplify things as easily applied principles. The heart and spirit can appear synonymous, yet in simplest terms, the heart deals with motivations. The most important of our considerations is self-centered motivations versus God-centered and people-oriented motivations. If our heart is not changed, it will influence the mind in an automatic mode that we will not always be able to discern. The pathway to becoming a true son of God will take you through the process of the "death of self" so that the spirit within you will be able to function as it once did.

Since my heart is deceitfully wicked, I should never assume I know my heart or anybody else's heart. I must see it as the territory of God. *He* will "give" us a new heart, the Word declares. It does not say *we* will "create" a new heart. What we can do is allow God to show us our hearts and then respond properly when He exposes our heart. We must always be looking for the most obvious error of the heart, which is the center of our motivations.

Why do you do the things that you do? That is not always an easy question to answer but the answer will give you a clue to your spiritual progress.

Once we realize the need for proper motivations in the heart, we are ready to take the next step to see how feelings impact our understanding. The use of knowledge without feeling will not produce true understanding. Man was created in perfect harmony, but with the fall, that harmony was broken. In Christ we are able to restore that harmony and allow all parts of our nature to function in perfect synchronization. We see how this works with the knowledge of the Word. Many people know the Word but make it a sword of destruction, not a sword of deliverance. Knowledge can be dangerous in the hands of angry men. Jesus demonstrated this in the story of the woman caught in the very act of adultery. The men of the city brought her and threw her at the feet of Jesus.

They said to Him, "Teacher, this woman was caught in adultery, in the very act. Now Moses, in the law, commanded us that such should be stoned. But what do You say?" (John 8:4-5)

They wanted to bring an accusation against Jesus. Look what Jesus did and said:

But Jesus stooped down and wrote on the ground with His finger, as though He did not hear. So when they continued asking Him, He raised Himself up and said to them, "He who is without sin among you, let him throw a stone at her first." And again He stooped down and wrote on the ground (John 8:6b-8).

The second time Jesus wrote on the ground He did so as a stalling tactic. He wanted those men to have time to get in touch with their feelings. He knew they needed to get in touch with their consciences. Look what happened next.

Then those who heard it, being convicted by their conscience, went out one by one, beginning with the oldest even to the last. And Jesus was left alone, and the woman standing in the midst (John 8:9).

To properly understand the Word of God, you have to be in touch with your feelings. To be a true son of God, like Jesus, you must put heart into the equation of your understanding. Unfortunately, the Church has too much knowledge and not enough heart.

If we follow the letter rather than the Spirit, we will actually stand in opposition to the purposes of God even when we think we are on His side. Jesus was not only in touch with His feelings, He was also in touch with the feelings of others. This is what the Bible calls compassion, a co-passion, which is feeling the pain and condition of another. True sons of God are able to identify with the pain of others. They have overcome the tendency towards self-absorption and are now easily touched by the conditions of those around them.

In the end Father's favor will rest upon those who have discovered His heart. The light of His glory shines powerfully though their own hearts and affects everything that they do. The mind of the spiritual son has been renewed and is now open to receive truth from the Spirit. Empowered by the heart of God and led by the mind of Christ, the Church can now go forth and mightily influence the world around her, and the favor of Father will be her glory.

Ministry Contact Information

Call From The Mountain Media Ministries
4900 Maybee Road
Clarkston, Michigan 48348
248.391.6166
www.mtzion.org

Additional copies of this book and other
book titles from DESTINY IMAGE are
available at your local bookstore.

For a bookstore near you, call 1-800-722-6774.

Send a request for a catalog to:

Destiny Image® Publishers, Inc.

P.O. Box 310
Shippensburg, PA 17257-0310

*"Speaking to the Purposes of God for This
Generation and for the Generations to Come"*

For a complete list of our titles,
visit us at www.destinyimage.com